First Edition, 2022

Tonya A. Brown
3436 Magazine St
#460
New Orleans, LA 70115
www.witchwaypublishing.com

Editor: Tonya A. Brown
Internal Design: Amanda Smith and Tonya A. Brown
Coloring Pages: Siobhan Duncan
Writers: Tonya A. Brown, Amanda Wilson, Zehara Nachash, Jessica Marie Baumgartner, S. Strange, Briony Silver, Luna Aliendro, Kiki Dombrowski.

ISBN 978-1-0880-0343-5

Please note that signs and moon phases can depend on your location, if this is a vital part of your practice, always check multiple references.

IF LOST, PLEASE RETURN TO:

_____

_____

_____

_____

DESIGN A SIGIL

A sigil, in short, is a magical symbol. Sigils are designed based on their intended goal. In this case, you will create a sigil specific to this planner. What it will do to or for the planner is up to you – typically sigils are used to protect or empower an object, so you could, for example, design a sigil to protect the planner from theft, loss, or damage.

Another option is to create a sigil that will enchant the planner, so it becomes a magical device that, for instance, enhances your productivity or boosts creativity. There's no wrong way to do this – it's your planner, and you should create a sigil that will serve you best. I have provided the steps for two different methods of sigil design to help you get started on your design.

Chaos Magic Method

Step 1. Compose a clear and concise statement of the intent of the sigil.

Step 2. Remove all the vowels and duplicate letters of the sentence.

Step 3. Combine the remaining letters to create the symbol.

Zakroff Method

I refer to this method as the Zakroff Method because it was created by Laura Tempest Zakroff. Compared to the Chaos magic method, Zakroff's method is designed to be more intuitive and fluid, and, according to Zakroff's "Sigil Witchery", it's "accessible to people with a wide variety of abilities and experiences."

Step 1. Identify your goal- what do you want the sigil to do?

Step 2. Brainstorm a list of what you'll need to achieve the goal. For example, if you want the sigil to protect your planner from becoming lost or damaged in any way, you'll come up with symbols to represent protection, the planner, and remaining whole and unharmed.

Step 3. Design the sigil. Find fun ways to put your favorite doodles together in a way that appeals to you aesthetically and magically.

Step 4. Apply the sigil – aka, draw the sigil on the Planner Sigil page. There is no need to charge the final design because the thought and energy put into the creation is more than sufficient to empower the final design.

INTENTION:

Your Diety Correspondences

If you were a diety, what would people use to represent you?

What spells would you be summoned to help with?

_____
_____
_____

Crystal, elements, foods, colors, flowers, & animal associations:

_____
_____
_____
_____
_____
_____

What chant would be used to summon you?:

_____
_____
_____
_____
_____
_____

Magically Managed Week

Monday

Ruled by the Moon. Associated with Lunar deities. Colors: silver, white, pale blue. Crystals: moonstone, pearl. Herbs/Plants: mint and plants of mint family (i.e., catnip), sage, chamomile. Monday is a day for family, friends, and fertility. The moon has a strong connection to intuition, so it's the perfect day for psychic awareness, as well as introspection.

Tuesday

Ruled by Mars. Named for Norse god Tyr, associated with gods of war, battle, sovereignty and conflict. Colors: red, orange. Crystals: rubies, garnet. Herbs/plants: thistle, coneflower. Tuesday passion and excitement makes for great sex magic, and workings to heal/strengthen marriages and partnerships. This is a day to stake your claim and make a name for yourself, using the energy of strategy and cunning.

Wednesday

Ruled by Mercury. Named for Norse god Woden. Color: purple. Crystals: aventurine, agate. Herbs/Plants: Aspen trees, lilies, lavender. Wednesday is the day to perform workings for the benefit of your business or career, plan trips and open lines of communication.

Thursday

Ruled by Jupiter. Associated with deities in leadership positions, such as Zeus, Jupiter, the Dagda. Colors: blues and greens. Crystals: turquoise, amethyst, lapis lazuli. Herbs/Plants: honeysuckle, cinquefoil, oak tree. Thursday has an energy of expansion, so money, success, and generosity are all excellent intentions for workings.

Friday

Ruled by Venus. Associated with Deities of love and beauty. Colors: pink, aqua. Crystals: coral, emerald. Herbs/Plants: strawberry, apple blossom, feverfew. Friday is the perfect day to work a glamour, enhancing and emphasizing upon your best qualities. It's a day for strengthening friendships, spicing up your love life.

Saturday

Ruled by Saturn. Associated with the goddess Hecate. Colors: black, purple. Crystals: obsidian, hematite. Herbs/Plants: thyme, Cypress tree. The last day of the week, naturally, generates energy of endings and, ironically, longevity. It's a day for honoring the household spirits, and workings to find a new home.

Sunday

Ruled by the Sun. Associated with Solar Deities. Colors: yellow, gold. Crystals: Quartz, diamond, carnelian, amber. Herbs/Plants: marigold, sunflower, cinnamon. Sunday is a day for workings that involve beauty, joy, and hope. Excellent day for when you need a victory, or to guarantee the successful start of something new.

Record a Card Pull

DECK USED:

_____

CARD(S) PULLED:

_____

_____

_____

YOUR INTERPRETATION:

_____

_____

_____

_____

_____

_____

_____

BOOK INTERPRETATION:

_____

_____

_____

_____

_____

_____

"If the plan doesn't work, change
the plan, but never the goal."

– Author Unknown

January

Calendar Key
- Full Moon
- New Moon
- First Quarter
- Last Quarter
- Eclipse
- Sun

DECEMBER

M	T	W	T	F	S	S
			1	2	3	4
5	6	7	8	9	10	11
12	13	14	15	16	17	18
19	20	21	22	23	24	25
26	27	28	29	30	31	

FEBRUARY

M	T	W	T	F	S	S
		1	2	3	4	5
6	7	8	9	10	11	12
13	14	15	16	17	18	19
20	21	22	23	24	25	26
27	28					

Goals

Notes

Monday	Tuesday	Wednesday
30 30/335	**31** 31/334	
2 02/363	**3** 03/362	**4** 04/361
9 09/356	**10** 10/355	**11** 11/354
16 16/349 Martin Luther King, Jr. Day	**17** 17/348	**18** 18/347
23 23/342 · · · **30**	**24** 24/341 · · · **31**	**25** 25/340

JANUARY

M	T	W	T	F	S	S
30	31					1
2	3	4	5	6	7	8
9	10	11	12	13	14	15
16	17	18	19	20	21	22
23	24	25	26	27	28	29

Thursday			Friday			Saturday			Sunday		
									1	01/364	New Year's Day
5	05/360		**6**	06/359		**7**	07/358		**8**	08/357	
12	12/353		**13**	13/352		**14**	14/351		**15**	15/350	
19	19/346		**20**	20/345		**21**	21/344		**22**	22/343	
26	26/339		**27**	27/338		**28**	28/337		**29**	29/336	

GOALS & DREAMS

6-MONTH PROJECT LIST

GOAL: _____ DUE DATE: _____

ENVISION YOUR LIFE AFTER OBTAINING YOUR GOAL.
HOW DO YOU FEEL?

_____

_____

_____

_____

_____

MONTHLY ACTION STEPS:

_____

_____

_____

_____

_____

NOTES:

_____

_____

_____

_____

RITUAL PLANNER

GOAL/INTENTION:

_____

_____

_____

ITEMS NEEDED:

_____

_____

_____

_____

_____

STEPS:

_____

_____

_____

_____

LUNAR PHASES

JANUARY 6TH: FULL MOON IN CANCER

The Moon in Cancer instills in you emotional security and a sense of belonging, a sense of nurturing you feel instinctively. You find that you're longing for an intimate connection that's meaningful and long-lasting, enough so you can establish a sense of belonging-put down roots, a place to bunker down as the Universe throws its' trials and tribulations at you. Using the Full Moon energies to work a self-love spell may help to satisfy this desire.

JANUARY 15TH: LAST QUARTER IN LIBRA

The last quarter in Libra is the perfect energy for establishing balance and harmony, particularly for wrapping up projects and tasks. The energy of the moon phase and the position provide a unique opportunity for bringing things to a close neatly, and in an orderly fashion, so you are free to move onto the next step or phase of your journey.

JANUARY 21ST: NEW MOON IN CAPRICORN

The moon in Capricorn has an emotional seriousness, a sober orientation, and a practical awareness that brings with it a need to feel useful. Using the energies of the new moon and amplified ambitions of Capricorn, this is an ideal time to start new projects.

JANUARY 28TH: FIRST QUARTER IN TAURUS

Your sense of safety arises from the need for stability which is difficult to find at the moment. The key to stability is acceptance – accepting that change is a part of life, and acceptance of who you are as a person. When you accept yourself you will find that peace and tranquility are much easier to come by in your daily life.

JANUARY HERB GUIDE

You will see that there is an Herb Planting Guide section for each month of 2023. The articles cover a range of topics, such as gardening techniques, herb suggestions, and many more. But before I go any further, I want to thank my friend and fellow writer, Kiki Dombrowski, for her help with preparing this guide.

It is thanks to her wise suggestions and creative ideas that I was able to provide you with such an interesting collection of articles. Kiki has been a witch since her teen years, and now writes about witchcraft extensively, including more than five years of writing for Witch Way Magazine. Follow Kiki on Twitter at @KiKiD33 or on Instagram at @kikiscauldron.

While witchcraft and nature go hand in hand, it doesn't mean that all witches are expert gardeners, so that is why the first couple of articles of the Herb Planting Guide are covering beginner basics- to give beginners a helping hand and experienced gardeners a refresher. This month is a simple list of common gardening terms.

Common Gardening Terms

Annual: a plant that completes its lifecycle in one year or less
Biennial: a plant that lives for 2 years.
Companion Planting: the practice of using a specific combination of plants growing together in order to provide a variety of benefits (i.e., attract pollinators, deter pests, etc.).
Compost: decomposed organic matter. (See March planting guide for more information)
Deadheading: removing a bloom past its' prime from the plant to encourage new growth
Direct Sow: planting the seed directly into the final growth location
Full Sun: a minimum of 6 hours of direct sunlight
Hardiness Zone: the US was grouped into sections and designated hardiness zone numbers based on climatic conditions to determine which plants will grow best in which areas of the country. To assess your Hardiness Zone, refer to the Hardiness Zone map in the Appendix.
Part Sun/Shade: 3-6 hours of sun a day
Perennial: a plant that lives 2 or more years

A TRUE RESET

It is the beginning of the year. What does this mean? Well, it means a lot of lofty goals, financial recouping from the holiday season, and shaking off the buzz of many events and social obligations.

A new year means that we can finally breathe again. While many websites, listicles, and magazines will tell you now is the time to kick it into gear with a new workout plan, a stricter budget, and new routines, we're going to be that friend that goes... hey witch, slow your roll. While yes, if you are feeling motivated, that's amazing. Work that flow and go with what you feel. However, I would feel like a bad friend if I didn't also gently remind you of the chaotic holiday season that you just went through. Indulge in a bit of self-care this January before you take on the year of 2023.

You may be thinking, "Oh great! Another article on taking a bubble bath. Pass." No, no, hear me out. While yes, if you think I'm not about to tell you to go take a bubble bath, you are crazy. Still, I'm also going to include some other ideas to make an actual refreshing start to your year and help you breathe a little easier. Let's talk about 3 fundamental aspects of your life that tend to get bogged down; your body, mind, and space.

Let's talk about your space.

A cluttered space makes us feel like we're spiraling. It is my own guilty habit, and it often makes me feel overwhelmed and out of control. So I'm going to give you a little homework to schedule into this planner. It will take no more than 30 minutes. Throw out all of those holiday leftovers. I know you're so sure that you're going to do something with that ham bone... but really... are you?

Next, you see that pile of gifts that have no home yet? I know you have no idea if you even like the lamp from Aunt Jo or the slow cooker from your mom that she also gave you a year ago. Take 20 minutes to go through them, give them homes, or decide if they need to be donated.

Finally, now is the perfect time to remove the holiday-specific items from your space. The tree, the Santa decor, and your ironic ugly Christmas sweater for office parties are more than ready to be put away.

Let's talk about your mind.

We've just been through a pretty hectic, though fun season. Parties, feasts, social events often clutter the holiday season, and sometimes we can feel a little overwhelmed. Try a few of these tasks to help unclutter the mind as you go into the new year. Spend about 45 minutes and clean up your inbox. Yes, the dreaded inbox. Deleted everything that is no longer useful and finally respond to the items you've been putting off. Clear out your DVR - yes, you've been recording all 7 seasons of Buffy, but if you've gone almost 3 months without watching a single episode, it's time for it to go. Finally, let us talk about emotions. The holiday season is full of complex emotional situations, and worrying about what your friend meant precisely when she made that comment or why your long-hated cousin was invited to a party, won't do you any good. Let's face it, you won't find answers. People are complicated. Let that shit go.

Let's talk about your body.

This is typically what we associate with self-care. First off, start the year off with a health check. If you are lucky enough to have insurance, get a physical. If not, take stock of any pains, discomforts, and other aspects of your body you may be concerned about.

Next, take about 15 minutes and treat yourself to a Guided Body Scan. This is a beautiful meditation. You can find multiple versions online, which will help you become more intuned with your body.

Now... I know you've been waiting for this part... destressing. Take some time for yourself to do acts of de-stress. Baths, face masks, grounding, meditation - whatever it is that makes you feel clear from tension and stress.

There we go witches, I hope this gives you a little extra motivation to begin the year off with a tabula rasa.

PAUSE & REFLECT

Take a moment and predict what you think this year will be like for you.

_____

_____

_____

_____

_____

_____

_____

_____

_____

_____

_____

_____

_____

_____

_____

_____

_____

_____

JANUARY FESTIVALS

In Benin, starting on the 10th of January, the country honors its ancestors and gods by celebrating the African spirituality, Vodoun (Voodoo). The holiday is celebrated across the whole country, but Ouidah is the epicenter of the festivities. The Fête du Vodoun, or the Vodoun Festival, is a beautiful way to celebrate a spirituality that has traveled world-wide, survived generations, and shaped communities far and wide. The festivities begin with the sacrificial slaughter of a goat to honor the spirits, and followed by joyous dancing, singing, and imbibing of liquor – particularly gin.

[Source: https://en.wikipedia.org/wiki/Fête du Vodoun]

USE THE SPACE BELOW TO RECORD YOUR JANUARY CELEBRATIONS

JANUARY

	M	T	W	T	F	S	S
52	26	27	28	29	30	31	1
1	2	3	4	5	6	7	8
2	9	10	11	12	13	14	15
3	16	17	18	19	20	21	22
4	23	24	25	26	27	28	29
5	30	31	1	2	3	4	5

TO DO LIST

-
-
-
-
-
-
-
-
-

DAILY CARD PULL

Monday

Tuesday

Wednesday

Thursday

Friday

Saturday

Sunday

MONDAY 26

TUESDAY 27

WEDNESDAY 28

THURSDAY 29

2023

FRIDAY	30		GOALS

SATURDAY	31	New Year's Eve	REMEMBER

- •
- •
- •
- •
- •
- •
- •

SUNDAY	1	New Year's Day	NOTES

HABITS	M	T	W	T	F	S	S	NEXT WEEK

JANUARY

	M	T	W	T	F	S	S
52	26	27	28	29	30	31	1
1	2	3	4	5	6	7	8
2	9	10	11	12	13	14	15
3	16	17	18	19	20	21	22
4	23	24	25	26	27	28	29
5	30	31	1	2	3	4	5

TO DO LIST

-
-
-
-
-
-
-
-
-

DAILY CARD PULL

Monday

Tuesday

Wednesday

Thursday

Friday

Saturday

Sunday

MONDAY 02

TUESDAY 03

WEDNESDAY 04

THURSDAY 05

2023

FRIDAY	06		GOALS

SATURDAY	07		REMEMBER

-
-
-
-
-
-
-

SUNDAY	08		NOTES

HABITS	M	T	W	T	F	S	S	NEXT WEEK

JANUARY

	M	T	W	T	F	S	S
52	26	27	28	29	30	31	1
1	2	3	4	5	6	7	8
2	9	10	11	12	13	14	15
3	16	17	18	19	20	21	22
4	23	24	25	26	27	28	29
5	30	31	1	2	3	4	5

TO DO LIST

-
-
-
-
-
-
-
-
-

DAILY CARD PULL

Monday

Tuesday

Wednesday

Thursday

Friday

Saturday

Sunday

MONDAY 09

TUESDAY 10

WEDNESDAY 11

THURSDAY 12

2023

FRIDAY	13	

SATURDAY	14	🌓 ♎

SUNDAY	15	

GOALS

REMEMBER

-
-
-
-
-
-
-

NOTES

HABITS

	M	T	W	T	F	S	S

NEXT WEEK

JANUARY

	M	T	W	T	F	S	S
52	26	27	28	29	30	31	1
1	2	3	4	5	6	7	8
2	9	10	11	12	13	14	15
3	16	17	18	19	20	21	22
4	23	24	25	26	27	28	29
5	30	31	1	2	3	4	5

TO DO LIST

-
-
-
-
-
-
-
-
-

DAILY CARD PULL

Monday

Tuesday

Wednesday

Thursday

Friday

Saturday

Sunday

MONDAY	16	Martin Luther King, Jr. Day

TUESDAY	17	

WEDNESDAY	18	

THURSDAY	19	

FRIDAY   20 ☀ ♒

GOALS

SATURDAY   21 ● ♑

REMEMBER

-
-
-
-
-
-
-

SUNDAY   22

NOTES

HABITS

	M	T	W	T	F	S	S

NEXT WEEK

JANUARY

	M	T	W	T	F	S	S
52	26	27	28	29	30	31	1
1	2	3	4	5	6	7	8
2	9	10	11	12	13	14	15
3	16	17	18	19	20	21	22
4	23	24	25	26	27	28	29
5	30	31	1	2	3	4	5

TO DO LIST

-
-
-
-
-
-
-
-
-

DAILY CARD PULL

Monday

Tuesday

Wednesday

Thursday

Friday

Saturday

Sunday

MONDAY 23

TUESDAY 24

WEDNESDAY 25

THURSDAY 26

2023

FRIDAY	27	

GOALS

SATURDAY	28	◑♉

REMEMBER
-
-
-
-
-
-
-
-

SUNDAY	29	

NOTES

HABITS	M	T	W	T	F	S	S

NEXT WEEK

GRATITUDE LIST

_____

_____

_____

_____

_____

_____

_____

MONTHLY TO-DO'S

_____

_____

_____

_____

_____

_____

_____

_____

_____

_____

TRY SOMETHING NEW

CRYSTALS: amazonite
Amazonite is referred to the "Stone of Hope" because it brings hope, optimism, and instills faith in all who wear it. The power of the stone comes from the element of water and works directly with the heart chakra, which makes it the perfect stone to cultivate self-love and confidence. This is the very same stone that once emboldened warriors and adorned pharaohs as they set off for the land of the dead –Amazonite was found on shields of Amazonian tribal warrior women from the 10th century BCE, and Amazonite inlays decorated King Tutankhamun's golden death mask.

CARD SPREAD
Goals spread: Card 1: Objective – Card 2: Resource – Card 3: Outcome

SPELL: realignment of personal energies
Make 1x7 piece puzzle with heavy weight paper, as simple or elaborate as you wish. The colors, from top to bottom, are white, violet, blue, green, yellow, orange, red. Once pieces are cut out and colored in, hold them to each corresponding power point (Chakra) on your body to charge them. White-Crown, Violet-Third Eye, Blue-Throat, Green-Heart, Yellow-Solar Plexus, Orange- Sacral, Red- Root. Put the puzzle together, envisioning your energies aligning as the puzzle goes together.

ENTITY
Send the intention of forging a new spiritual alliance out into the universe, specifying how the spirit will get your attention. Start each day with this proclamation for a week. Pay attention for the sign in the weeks to come.

SELF-CARE
Clean and organize your desk/work area. Throw away scraps of paper, broken binder clips, receipts from 2018, wipe down the surfaces, and organize your supplies.

TEA: matcha tea
You may combine tea magic with other techniques to strengthen your working – i.e., choose your mug based on color magic, attach a crystal to the handle of the spoon used to stir the tea, draw symbols on the side of the mug with washable marker, etc.

HERBS: cinnamon
Cinnamon can help in spellwork with success, prosperity, good luck. The scent of cinnamon excellent for achieving a meditative state.

Record a Card Pull

DECK USED:

_____

CARD(S) PULLED:

_____

_____

_____

YOUR INTERPRETATION:

_____

_____

_____

_____

_____

_____

BOOK INTERPRETATION:

_____

_____

_____

_____

_____

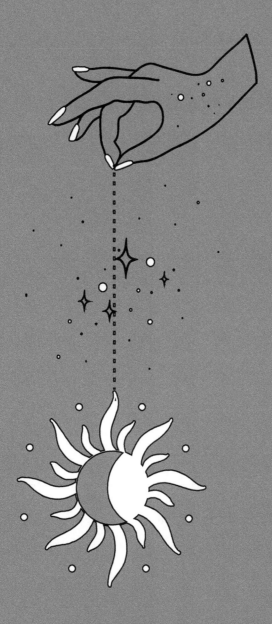

"Don't think about making art, just get it done. Let everyone else decide if it's good or bad, whether they love it or hate it. While they are deciding, make even more art."

- Andy Warhol

February

Full Moon   First Quarter   Eclipse

New Moon   Last Quarter   Sun

JANUARY

M	T	W	T	F	S	S
30	31					1
2	3	4	5	6	7	8
9	10	11	12	13	14	15
16	17	18	19	20	21	22
23	24	25	26	27	28	29

MARCH

M	T	W	T	F	S	S
		1	2	3	4	5
6	7	8	9	10	11	12
13	14	15	16	17	18	19
20	21	22	23	24	25	26
27	28	29	30	31		

Goals

Notes

Monday	Tuesday	Wednesday
		1 32/333 Imbo
6 37/328	**7** 38/327	**8** 39/326
13 44/321	**14** 45/320 Valentine's Day	**15** 46/319
20 51/314 Presidents' Day	**21** 52/313	**22** 53/312 Ash Wednesd
27 58/307	**28** 59/306	

FEBRUARY

M	T	W	T	F	S	S
		1	2	3	4	5
6	7	8	9	10	11	12
13	14	15	16	17	18	19
20	21	22	23	24	25	26
27	28					

Thursday	Friday	Saturday	Sunday
2 33/332	**3** 34/331	**4** 35/330	**5** 36/329
9 40/325	**10** 41/324	**11** 42/323	**12** 43/322
16 47/318	**17** 48/317	**18** 49/316	**19** 50/315
23 54/311	**24** 55/310	**25** 56/309	**26** 57/308

LUNAR PHASES

FEBRUARY 5TH: FULL MOON IN LEO

Impressing others and receiving praise will give you a sense of safety and security while the moon is in Leo. This only sets you up for failure, as you'll find yourself at a loss as soon as you're put in the spotlight. The key to navigating through Leo is accepting that feedback and criticism are useful, they help you improve. The first step to accepting these facts is to admit you are afraid of criticism, and to admit that you can't accept criticism. Only once you admit the truth of the problem can you work through it.

FEBRUARY 13TH: LAST QUARTER IN SCORPIO

Scorpio energy encourages us to explore our feelings more deeply and helps us evaluate things in our life more objectively. This time is best utilized to move away from that which no longer serves, especially when it comes to shallow relationships that aren't beneficial for the parties involved.

FEBRUARY 20TH: NEW MOON IN PISCES

Under the Gemini moon you may find that communicating your feelings and emotions becomes easier. Your actions are motivated by the desire for variety and the urge to satisfy curiosity. Just be careful you don't become reckless and fickle – the key is harmony of the mind and heart.

FEBRUARY 27TH: FIRST QUARTER IN GEMINI

Under the Gemini moon you may find that communicating your feelings and emotions becomes easier. Your actions are motivated by the desire for variety and the urge to satisfy curiosity. Just be careful you don't become reckless and fickle – the key is harmony of the mind and heart.

RITUAL PLANNER

GOAL/INTENTION:

_____

_____

_____

ITEMS NEEDED:

_____

_____

_____

_____

STEPS:

_____

_____

_____

_____

FEBRUARY HERBS

Gardening can be relatively simple- it's a matter of caring
and crooning to plants. It becomes quite vexing if you don't
thoughtfully plan your garden and end up with sick and/or dying
plants. Choose the plants you wish to grow, keeping in mind the
Hardiness Zone, sun exposure and soil type.

Next you'll determine the gardening method, (See July Herb
Planting Guide for more information about garden layouts), where
in your yard the garden will go, and then design the garden. Each
plant is unique, so a major part of gardening is taking the time
to learn about each one. It's important to remember your plants
are living beings that crave love, support, encouragement, and
attention.

HERB	SIZE/ SPREAD	START SEEDS IN-SIDE/OUTSIDE	HARDINESS ZONE	NATIVE REGION	GROWTH TYPE**	SUN, SOIL
Cilantro/ Coriander	12"2'/2"-1.5'	Direct Sow in Fall	8-10	Southern Europe, Western Mediterranean	A	FS/W
Chives	12-18"	8-10 after/3-4 before	3-10	Temperate areas of Europe, Asia, North America	P	FS/RM
Lemon Balm	12-24"/12-24"	8 before-last frost	4-9	South-central Europe, Mediterranean Basin, Iran, Central Asia	P	FS/W S
Sage	12-48"-30"	6-10 before/1-2 before	5-8	Mediterraneean	P	FS/W

*Weeks before or afer last spring frost

** A=Annual P=Perennial

** FS= full sun, PS= partial sun; WD= well-drained, M= moist, RM, rich moint, L= loamy, LS=loamy/sandy

EXPLORING TYPES OF LOVE

During the season of love, it's easy to get caught up in only one version of what love can look like. Romantic! It's what fueled the early 2000s with rom-coms ruling supreme, and it is so indoctrinated into our society that even witches hear *love spells*, and scoff, making their own closed-minded assumptions. So, this month, let's explore different types of love, according to the ancient Greeks.

1. Eros (sexual passion) – This is sexual, a love that is physical and between lovers. Paired with Pragma, this can be a recipe for an amazing romance, but just on its own, Eros can be a wonderful and powerful experience. A whirlwind fling is what movies are made of.

2. Philia (deep friendship) – This is friendship, the love two people feel for each other that is about comradery and shared experiences. This is often a love that can be very painful when it ends, as it feels the utmost personal, yet we often don't view it as important as we should.

3. Ludus (playful love) – New love, puppy love, flirty love. This is that 'love at first sight' feeling, the initial spark of something exciting. Often based on nothing more than chemicals or limited experience, Ludas love has the potential to turn into any of the other types of love.

4. Agape (love for everyone) – This is love for others in the most broadest sense. Love for people, the world, or groups of people. I imagine this is the love women in a club form in the bathrooms. The "I don't know you, but you're so perfect, pretty, and incredible" – It's love for others based off of no conditions. Spiritually, people relate this as love between deity and human. Paired with Storge, this can represent the unconditional love a parent feels for a child.

5. Pragma (longstanding love) – Pragma love is one that can withstand the rest of time, love that persists and is deeply imbedded and at this point unbreakable. Paired with Philia this can be long-life friends, paired with Eros and Ludus we would call it soulmates. Often this is knowing someone to the core, and loving them harder for it.

6. Philautia (love of the self) – Self love! This is loving ourselves and this is one of the hardest loves to obtain. Caring for ourselves as if we're someone else is often difficult and a lifelong challenge for some. Appreciating and loving your talents, skills, and taking care of ourselves is a valuable, needed love.

7. Storge (family love) – Familial love, this is the love we feel for our family members and our community. This is love based on need, survival, and shared existence. Through hard roads, time, and appreciation, family love is a powerful experience, whether it is family we are born to or family that we choose.

8. Mania (obsessive love) – This love is exactly as it sounds, often unhealthy and based off little, mania is a love we form for others that is fueled not by them, but our own perceptions, projections, and trauma. Paired with Eros or Ludas, this is what we see when people love someone they don't know, or only know briefly. I would call this love for our own idea of who someone else is, and not love for the actual person themselves.

So dear witch, now that you know these different types of love, not only can we do away with all the misconceptions we have about love spells, but we can also identify and appreciate all the different types of love that exist.

PAUSE & REFLECT

Name a form of divination that you would like to learn more about.
Summarize it here.

_____

_____

_____

_____

_____

_____

_____

_____

_____

_____

_____

_____

_____

_____

_____

_____

_____

FEBRUARY FESTIVALS

For the first two weeks of February every year, Easter Island carries out the Tapati Rapa Nui Festival. This cultural festival was established in the 1970's in order to maintain and promote the Rapa Nui culture, helping to generate interest and a 'sense of identity' in people, especially kids. From February 1st to the 15th, the island is abuzz with competitions, singing, dancing, and a number of sporting events. One remarkable sporting event they have is haka pei, where you sit on a banana tree trunk and slide down the island's steepest slope. Each event carries a certain number of points, which are used in the competition for the Queen of Tapati. Two women are selected as candidates, and they compete in each of the sporting events – Haka Pei, the island triathlon, swimming, canoeing, and horse racing. The woman with the most points at the end is crowned Queen. [Source: easterislandspirit.com]

USE THE SPACE BELOW TO RECORD YOUR FEBRUARY CELEBRATIONS

GRATITUDE LIST

_____

_____

_____

_____

_____

_____

_____

_____

MONTHLY TO-DO'S

_____

_____

_____

_____

_____

_____

_____

_____

_____

_____

_____

TRY SOMETHING NEW

CRYSTAL:
If you're not keen on using crystals in the form of raw or tumbled stones, you could explore using crystals in the form of jewelry. You could purchase rings with pearl, moonstone, ruby, or emerald, bracelets adorned with turquoise or jade, or you can make your own jewelry or keychains.

CARD SPREAD
Self-love spread: Card 1: Quality overlooked – Card 2: Quality/skill to hone – Card 3: Flaw to forget

SPELL: cleanse & clear heart energies
This is a spell for willing to accept love for oneself. May be done without tools, but a piece of rose quartz may help with directing the energy. Close your eyes, envision the power center in the middle of your chest. It's a spinning cube, shining a rosy, pink light. It may be cloudy, or dull. Maybe it has smudges. As it spins it becomes clear, shining brighter and brighter. Bask in the warm, loving light a few moments, then imagine the light fading out and the cube slowing to a stop to 'close' the chakra/power point.

ENTITY
Learn more about who you're descended from. You can find out a lot from Ancestry.com – for free (access to Census records, photos, etc.). If a name stands out to you try to initiate contact at your ancestor altar, (personal protections in place, using practices you're familiar with).

SELF-CARE
Write a love poem...about yourself. If you need a little help getting started, imagine it's a poem you would love to receive from the love-of-you-life/dream partner.

TEA: the love witch blend
Comprised of black tea, freeze-dried strawberries, rose petals, and a decadent chocolate blend, Chocolate Strawberry tea is a love spell in a cup. Made for the most powerful of love witches, bringing together the love magic of roses, the wisdom of chocolate, the sweetness of the strawberries and the strength of the black tea.

HERBS: damiana
This herb originates in Central and South America, its' usage dating back to that of the Mayans and Aztecs. Its primary use has been, and continues to be, to enhance sexual performance, vitality, and reproductive health in both men and women. Now, there have not been many studies conducted testing the efficacy and safety of this herb, so I would advise caution before ingesting or using the herb on your body -but that doesn't mean it cannot be used in spells, (i.e., to dress candles, add to spell jars, etc.).

FEBRUARY

	M	T	W	T	F	S	S
5	30	31	1	2	3	4	5
6	6	7	8	9	10	11	12
7	13	14	15	16	17	18	19
8	20	21	22	23	24	25	26
9	27	28	1	2	3	4	5

TO DO LIST

-
-
-
-
-
-
-
-
-

DAILY CARD PULL

Monday

Tuesday

Wednesday

Thursday

Friday

Saturday

Sunday

MONDAY 30

TUESDAY 31

WEDNESDAY 01 Imbolc

THURSDAY 02

2023

FRIDAY	03	

GOALS

SATURDAY 04

REMEMBER

-
-
-
-
-
-
-

SUNDAY 05

NOTES

HABITS	M	T	W	T	F	S	S

NEXT WEEK

FEBRUARY

	M	T	W	T	F	S	S
5	30	31	1	2	3	4	5
6	6	7	8	9	10	11	12
7	13	14	15	16	17	18	19
8	20	21	22	23	24	25	26
9	27	28	1	2	3	4	5

TO DO LIST

-
-
-
-
-
-
-
-
-

DAILY CARD PULL

Monday

Tuesday

Wednesday

Thursday

Friday

Saturday

Sunday

○

MONDAY | 06

TUESDAY | 07

WEDNESDAY | 08

THURSDAY | 09

2023

FRIDAY	10	

GOALS

SATURDAY	11	

REMEMBER
-
-
-
-
-
-
-

SUNDAY	12	

NOTES

HABITS

	M	T	W	T	F	S	S

NEXT WEEK

FEBRUARY

	M	T	W	T	F	S	S
5	30	31	1	2	3	4	5
6	6	7	8	9	10	11	12
7	13	14	15	16	17	18	19
8	20	21	22	23	24	25	26
9	27	28	1	2	3	4	5

TO DO LIST

-
-
-
-
-
-
-
-
-

DAILY CARD PULL

Monday

Tuesday

Wednesday

Thursday

Friday

Saturday

Sunday

MONDAY	13	☾ ♏

TUESDAY	14	Valentine's Day

WEDNESDAY	15	

THURSDAY	16	

2023

FRIDAY	17	

GOALS

SATURDAY	18	

REMEMBER

-
-
-
-
-
-
-

SUNDAY	19 ☀)-(	

NOTES

HABITS	M	T	W	T	F	S	S

NEXT WEEK

FEBRUARY

	M	T	W	T	F	S	S
5	30	31	1	2	3	4	5
6	6	7	8	9	10	11	12
7	13	14	15	16	17	18	19
8	20	21	22	23	24	25	26
9	27	28	1	2	3	4	5

TO DO LIST

-
-
-
-
-
-
-
-
-

DAILY CARD PULL

Monday

Tuesday

Wednesday

Thursday

Friday

Saturday

Sunday

MONDAY · 20 ● ♓

TUESDAY · 21

WEDNESDAY · 22

THURSDAY · 23

2023

FRIDAY 24

GOALS

SATURDAY 25

REMEMBER

-
-
-
-
-
-
-

SUNDAY 26

NOTES

HABITS

	M	T	W	T	F	S	S

NEXT WEEK

Record a Card Pull

DECK USED:
_____

CARD(S) PULLED:
_____
_____

YOUR INTERPRETATION:
_____
_____
_____
_____
_____

BOOK INTERPRETATION:
_____
_____
_____
_____
_____

want to be around people that do things. I don't want to be around
eople anymore that judge or talk about what people do. I want to be
around people that dream and support and do things."

- Amy Poehler

March

Calendar Key

🌕 Full Moon   🌓 First Quarter   🌘 Eclipse

🌑 New Moon   🌗 Last Quarter   ☀ Sun

FEBRUARY

M	T	W	T	F	S	S
		1	2	3	4	5
6	7	8	9	10	11	12
13	14	15	16	17	18	19
20	21	22	23	24	25	26
27	28					

APRIL

M	T	W	T	F	S	S
					1	2
3	4	5	6	7	8	9
10	11	12	13	14	15	16
17	18	19	20	21	22	23
24	25	26	27	28	29	30

Goals

Notes

_____
_____
_____
_____
_____
_____
_____
_____
_____
_____
_____
_____
_____

Monday	Tuesday	Wednesday
		1 60/305
6 65/300	**7** 66/299 🌕♍	**8** 67/298
13 72/293	**14** 73/292	**15** 74/291 🌗♐
20 79/286 Spring Equinox	**21** 80/285 🌑♓ ☀♈	**22** 81/284
27 86/279	**28** 87/278	**29** 88/277 🌓♋

MARCH

M	T	W	T	F	S	S
		1	2	3	4	5
6	7	8	9	10	11	12
13	14	15	16	17	18	19
20	21	22	23	24	25	26
27	28	29	30	31		

Thursday	Friday	Saturday	Sunday
2 61/304	3 62/303	4 63/302	5 64/301
9 68/297	10 69/296	11 70/295	12 71/294
16 75/290	17 76/289 St. Patrick's Day	18 77/288	19 78/287
23 82/283	24 83/282	25 84/281	26 85/280
30 89/276	31 90/275		

LUNAR PHASES

MARCH 7TH: FULL MOON IN VIRGO

The Virgo moon is one of order and practicality. You feel you have to reorganize and bring order to anything you feel is in chaos. This can lead to being intolerant of others, so try focusing more on solving problems, creating order within your life, and helping others without judgement.

MARCH 15TH: LAST QUARTER IN SAGITTARIUS

The energy of the waning moon in Sagittarius enables you to release that which no longer serves you, freeing you to start the next cycle with a clean slate.

MARCH 21ST: NEW MOON IN PISCES

The moon in Pisces is a great time for a creative or spiritual quest, as the energy heightens your emotional sensitivity and perception of your surroundings. Be mindful of feelings of insecurity. Should you begin to feel insecure just be patient and open to letting events unfold as they come.

MARCH 29TH: FIRST QUARTER IN CANCER

The Moon in Cancer instills in you emotional security and a sense of belonging, a sense of nurturing you feel instinctively. You find that you're longing for an intimate connection that's meaningful and long-lasting, enough so you can establish a sense of belonging-put down roots, a place to bunker down as the Universe throws its' trials and tribulations at you. Using the Full Moon energies to work a self-love spell may help to satisfy this desire..

RITUAL PLANNER

GOAL/INTENTION:

_____

_____

_____

ITEMS NEEDED:

_____

_____

_____

_____

_____

STEPS:

_____

_____

_____

_____

MARCH HERB PLANTING GUIDE: DIY COMPOST

Compost, simply put, is decomposed organic material. You could buy compost, but making your own homemade compost saves money, supports the environment, and provides your garden with nutrients infused with your positive energies. According to the EPA website, composting requires three basic ingredients: Browns, Greens, and Water. Browns provide carbon and consist of things like dead leaves, twigs, branches. Greens provide nitrogen, consisting of things like grass clippings, tea bags coffee grounds, eggshells, fruit scraps, and vegetable waste. Add enough water to make the material moist, which helps break down the organic matter. The compost should have an equal amount of browns to greens, and the layers should alternate between organic matter and different-sized particles.

You'll need a plastic bin with a lid. The recommended size is 18 gallons or larger. Drill 8-10 holes 1-2" apart in the bottom of the bin and in the lid. Put first bin inside a second bin if you want to collect and save the liquid (aka compost tea) leaking from the bottom of the first. Decide where the compost bin will be kept (on the porch, outside the kitchen window, in a shed, next to the garden, etc) and get it into position. You'll add the material in layers, adding water between each layer to moisten any dry material. Lay down the base material, ie. shredded newspaper, dried leaves, until the bin is about a quarter of the way full. Add dirt until the bin is about half full. Add scraps and other compostable material. Make sure the scraps are small in size to make decomposition easier – cut up the food scraps, rinse and crush the egg shells, tear up the napkins and paper towels.

With a small shovel stir the contents, folding them into each other. Make sure the compost is moist but not soggy and secure the lid. Every day the bin should be shaken up a bit to make sure air is flowing through the entire bin. If it's too moist, add shredded leaves, sawdust, or newspaper to soak up excess water. Alternatively, if the material is too dry, use a spray bottle to dampen the material. Keep a bin or bag in the kitchen to collect food scraps that you'll add to the compost bin every week or so, along with twigs and leaves and such to maintain the green to brown ratio. Compost will be ready in 2-3 months. You'll know it's ready because it will be a soft, dark, soil-like material. Use it as mulch or mix with soil to fertilize your garden.

Resources:
https://www.epa.gov/recycle/composting-home
https://www.thespruce.com/compost-bin-from-plastic-storage-container-2539493
https://www.younghouselove.com/younghouselovedotcompost/

MAGICAL SPRING CLEANING

By S. Strange

It's the time of year to do our spring cleaning. This tradition is based on both ritual and biology. In the winter, the days are colder and it gets dark sooner so we generally don't have much energy. Once the days become longer again, we are filled with extra energy, which we like to use to refreshen and renew ourselves just as nature does around us.

While we are sweeping and cleaning is the perfect time to add some magical touches and protection to our home. I want to elaborate on a few simple things you can do while cleaning that will also renew your home spiritually. My goal is to do this without adding a ton of extra work to your cleaning routine, so I try to combine things I already do with magical touches.

Clean Yourself First

The first step to a spiritually clean house is making sure you are spreading positive energy as you are going about your cleaning. To do this, take a moment to cleanse yourself before you start. You can do this by taking a shower and imagining any stress and negativity being washed off you. You can also go outside and do some grounding beforehand. While you clean, you want the good energy to persist, so try to make the activity fun. Put on some music to get into a positive mental zone or try making the activity fun by doing a cleaning game. You can easily assign yourself tasks by using existing tarot cards and assigning each card an activity or by creating your own cleaning oracle cards to tell you what to do next. You can also write tasks or areas on pieces of paper and then draw them out of your cauldron or write a list and have the dice decide which task to tackle first.

Positive Tools Spread Positive Energy

In addition to having yourself spread positive energy, you want to make sure that your cleaning utensils do the same. Swap out cleaning materials that have seen better days and recharge them by putting them under the full moon to soak up all the good energy. Once you prep your tools, they will help you spread positive energy every time you use them!

Add Magical Herbs

Now that you and your tools are ready, let's add some magic to our cleaning solutions by using herbs or essential oils. You can soak herbs in plain olive oil to create your own magical oil or use essential oils. You can add those to your regular cleaning solutions or use cleaning solutions that already include essential oils to cut down on that step. Lemon and peppermint, both in herb and essential oil form, are great for cleaning because they not only have magical cleaning properties, but they smell good too! But choose any herb or essential oil that offers what you need. It doesn't always have to be about cleaning properties, you can also choose one based on a need you have in your life or home.

If you have a carpet, you can mix your oils with baking soda and spread this out over the carpet prior to vacuuming. If you use a Swiffer, you can add a few drops to your sheet. You can also mix the oils with water and alcohol to make your own cleaning solution for surfaces and windows.

Intention is Everything

While sweeping or mopping, focus on spreading positive energy and cleaning off or sweeping out any negative energy. Be intentional in your cleaning. Once your surfaces are clean, don't forget to also clean the air by letting in fresh energy and sending negative energy out. This is a great time to take a moment to give your entrances and exits some special attention. Using salt in the form of a spray or sprinkled along the windowsill or stoop can help keep negative energies out. After all, you want your home to stay magically clean after you're done. Of course, you can also use a burning stick or cleanse the air if you choose. If you do not like to work with the smoke, try using a room spray made of alcohol and essential oils instead.

Take It a Step Further

After all this, you should have a physically and energetically clean home. Now it is up to you if you want to take this a few steps further and add a few touches to help keep the positive energy. While doing this, always think about the modes of entry into your home. You already cleaned the windows and doorways, but you can easily bring negativity in with you, so be conscious of releasing negative energy before reentering your home. You can do this by grounding or by dipping your fingers into a bowl of salt water that you keep at your entrance and taking a moment to release any negativity into the water (make sure to swap out the water regularly). Also think about the mail you bring in with you and take a moment to clean your mailbox to avoid bringing anything in with the mail. Adding some small bells to your front porch can also help protect the house and any packages that may be dropped off there.

Happy cleaning!

PAUSE & REFLECT

Do you follow the wheel of the year? If so, what if your favorite holiday? If not, make one up here.

_____

_____

_____

_____

_____

_____

_____

_____

_____

_____

_____

_____

_____

_____

_____

_____

_____

_____

_____

MARCH FESTIVALS

One of the most celebrated festivals in India is Holi. Holi is an enthusiastically celebrated ancient Hindu festival that lasts for a day and a night. The lighting of the ritual bon fire the night before signifies the start to the festival the following day, serving as a symbol of the triumph of good over evil. Holi is about respect, love, and friendship. Holi is known as the Festival of Colors, named for the tradition of 'playing with colors', when adults and children alike gather in the streets to smear vibrantly colored gulal on one another and splash each other with brightly colored water, or throw water balloons filled with colored water at each other. In addition to playing with colors, Holi is celebrated by dancing, singing, eating of sweets, giving of gifts, and honoring of the gods.
[Source: https://www.holifestival.org/festival-of-colours.html]

USE THE SPACE BELOW TO RECORD YOUR MARCH CELEBRATIONS

MARCH

	M	T	W	T	F	S	S
9	27	28	1	2	3	4	5
10	6	7	8	9	10	11	12
11	13	14	15	16	17	18	19
12	20	21	22	23	24	25	26
13	27	28	29	30	31	1	2

TO DO LIST

-
-
-
-
-
-
-
-
-

DAILY CARD PULL

Monday

Tuesday

Wednesday

Thursday

Friday

Saturday

Sunday

MONDAY	27	☽ ♊

TUESDAY	28	

WEDNESDAY	01	

THURSDAY	02	

2023

FRIDAY 03

GOALS

SATURDAY 04

REMEMBER

-
-
-
-
-
-
-

SUNDAY 05

NOTES

HABITS

	M	T	W	T	F	S	S

NEXT WEEK

MARCH

	M	T	W	T	F	S	S
9	27	28	1	2	3	4	5
10	6	7	8	9	10	11	12
11	13	14	15	16	17	18	19
12	20	21	22	23	24	25	26
13	27	28	29	30	31	1	2

TO DO LIST

-
-
-
-
-
-
-
-
-

DAILY CARD PULL

	Monday
	Tuesday
	Wednesday
	Thursday
	Friday
	Saturday
	Sunday

MONDAY 06

TUESDAY 07 🌑 ♍

WEDNESDAY 08

THURSDAY 09

2023

FRIDAY	10		GOALS

SATURDAY	11		REMEMBER

REMEMBER
-
-
-
-
-
-
-

SUNDAY	12	Daylight Saving Time Begins	NOTES

HABITS	M	T	W	T	F	S	S	NEXT WEEK

MARCH

	M	T	W	T	F	S	S
9	27	28	1	2	3	4	5
10	6	7	8	9	10	11	12
11	13	14	15	16	17	18	19
12	20	21	22	23	24	25	26
13	27	28	29	30	31	1	2

TO DO LIST

-
-
-
-
-
-
-
-
-

DAILY CARD PULL

Monday

Tuesday

Wednesday

Thursday

Friday

Saturday

Sunday

MONDAY 13

TUESDAY 14

WEDNESDAY 15

THURSDAY 16

2023

FRIDAY	17	St. Patrick's Day

GOALS

SATURDAY	18

REMEMBER

-
-
-
-
-
-
-

SUNDAY	19

NOTES

HABITS	M	T	W	T	F	S	S

NEXT WEEK

MARCH

	M	T	W	T	F	S	S
9	27	28	1	2	3	4	5
10	6	7	8	9	10	11	12
11	13	14	15	16	17	18	19
12	20	21	22	23	24	25	26
13	27	28	29	30	31	1	2

TO DO LIST

-
-
-
-
-
-
-
-
-

DAILY CARD PULL

Monday

Tuesday

Wednesday

Thursday

Friday

Saturday

Sunday

MONDAY 20   Spring Equinox

TUESDAY 21 ●♓ ☀♈

WEDNESDAY 22

THURSDAY 23

2023

FRIDAY	24		GOALS

SATURDAY	25		REMEMBER

-
-
-
-
-
-
-

SUNDAY	26		NOTES

HABITS	M	T	W	T	F	S	S	NEXT WEEK

MARCH

	M	T	W	T	F	S	S
9	27	28	1	2	3	4	5
10	6	7	8	9	10	11	12
11	13	14	15	16	17	18	19
12	20	21	22	23	24	25	26
13	27	28	29	30	31	1	2

TO DO LIST

-
-
-
-
-
-
-
-
-

WEEK FOCUS

PRIORITIES

- ○
- ○
- ○
- ○
- ○
- ○
- ○

MONDAY 27

TUESDAY 28

WEDNESDAY 29

THURSDAY 30

2023

FRIDAY	31	

GOALS

SATURDAY | 01 |

REMEMBER
-
-
-
-
-
-
-

SUNDAY | 02 |

NOTES

HABITS

	M	T	W	T	F	S	S

NEXT WEEK

GRATITUDE LIST

MONTHLY TO-DO'S

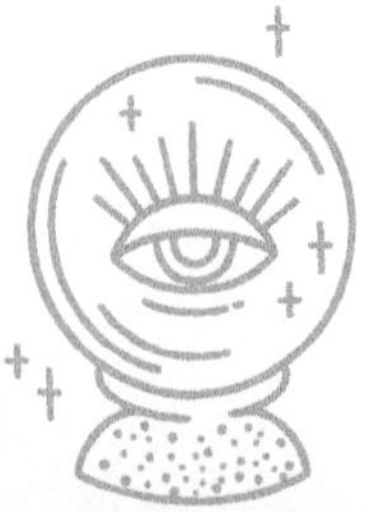

TRY SOMETHING NEW

CRYSTALS: bloodstone
Bloodstone is a dark green variation of chalcedony quartz with brownish-red spots of iron oxide. The blood-like hue of the iron oxide is what earned the stone its' name. The stone has been used for thousands of years, to instill strength – particularly to avoid being tricked or overwhelmed by malicious spirits, enhance courage, and cultivate self-confidence, making the stone excellent for magic concerning wealth and success.

CARD SPREAD
1: Love it - **Card 2:** Leave it - **Card 3:** Learn it

SPELL:
Spring is the time of growth, so work magic that builds with time. The perfect technique for a spell like this would be a living terrarium spell, using succulents, moss, or crystals. Bolster the spell using color, crystal, or sigil magic.

ENTITY
Tarot and oracle decks are excellent tools to utilize when working with, or seeking, an entity. The cards may represent a higher power in particular, or the archetype that a deity falls under. They can teach you about the entity, serve as representations in ritual, and even work as offerings for entities you're already working with.

SELF-CARE
Give yourself a manicure- I don't care if you've never touched an emery board before, it's time to start. Wash your hands with soap and dry thoroughly. Put Vaseline or cuticle oil on your cuticles, clip and file your nails so they're even and smooth. Rub your favorite lotion, taking care to massage your palms, wrists, and each finger.

TEA:
If you wish to try tea magic, but don't care for the taste of tea, you can experiment with this technique through alternative uses of the tea. Use it as a hair rinse, add it to bath water, use it to clean your hands, or apply it to a surface with a spray bottle, paint brush, or simply dipping your finger in the liquid and drawing what you wish (make sure the tea has cooled before attempting any working that entails the tea coming into contact with your skin).

HERBS
Basil is a versatile herb, with strong ties to money, success, wealth, and prosperity. It is a popular herb in love magic and has been said to ease temperament as well. This hardy plant has been in use for over 5000 years. The Greek word for basil translates to 'king' or 'royal', which explains why it's often referred to as the "King of Herbs".

APRIL FESTIVALS

The Parrtjima (parr-chee-ma) Festival in Alice Springs Australia is a free 10-day event that uses the newest technology to celebrate the world's oldest living culture, making this authentic Aboriginal festival is the only one of its' kind. The Arrernte people of Alice Springs host the Parrtjima Festival to display their artwork and, more importantly, educate people about their culture. During the day, visitors are encouraged to immerse themselves in the schedule of events, participating in interactive workshops, attending talks and discussions, viewing art created by local artists. The energies transform after night fall, as the mountains become illuminated by vibrant light shows, and live music echoes across the desert while people dance and celebrate. [Source: https://www.australia.com/en-us/events/arts-culture-and-music/parrtjima-festival.html]

USE THE SPACE BELOW TO RECORD YOUR APRIL CELEBRATIONS

"The problem with knowledge, is its inexhaustible craving. the more of it you have, the less you feel you know."

- Olivie Blake

April

MARCH

M	T	W	T	F	S	S
		1	2	3	4	5
6	7	8	9	10	11	12
13	14	15	16	17	18	19
20	21	22	23	24	25	26
27	28	29	30	31		

MAY

M	T	W	T	F	S	S
1	2	3	4	5	6	7
8	9	10	11	12	13	14
15	16	17	18	19	20	21
22	23	24	25	26	27	28
29	30	31				

Goals

Notes

Monday	Tuesday	Wednesday
3 93/272	**4** 94/271	**5** 95/270
10 100/265	**11** 101/264	**12** 102/263
17 107/258	**18** 108/257	**19** 109/256
24 114/251	**25** 115/250	**26** 116/249

APRIL

M	T	W	T	F	S	S
					1	2
3	4	5	6	7	8	9
10	11	12	13	14	15	16
17	18	19	20	21	22	23
24	25	26	27	28	29	30

Thursday	Friday	Saturday	Sunday
		1 91/274	**2** 92/273 Palm Sunday
6 96/269 ♌	**7** 97/268 Good Friday	**8** 98/267	**9** 99/266 Easter
13 103/262 ♑	**14** 104/261	**15** 105/260	**16** 106/259
20 110/255 ♉ ☀♉	**21** 111/254	**22** 112/253 Earth Day	**23** 113/252
27 117/248	**28** 118/247 ♌	**29** 119/246	**30** 120/245

LUNAR PHASES

APRIL 6TH: FULL MOON IN LIBRA

The moon in Libra drives us for a sense of order, but unlike that of the moon in Virgo, we are satisfied by pleasant interactions and aesthetics in the environment. The need for order and harmony are strong, and rather than deal with confrontation you try to keep everything 'nice'. Don't let the Libra moon make you forget who you are, and certainly resist the urge to bottle up your feelings.

APRIL 13TH: LAST QUARTER IN CAPRICORN

The moon in Capricorn has an emotional seriousness, a sober orientation, and a practical awareness that brings with it a need to feel useful. Using the energies of the new moon and amplified ambitions of Capricorn, this is an ideal time to start new projects.

APRIL 20TH: NEW MOON IN TAURUS (**SOLAR ECLIPSE**)

Your sense of safety arises from the need for stability which is difficult to find at the moment. The key to stability is acceptance – accepting that change is a part of life, and acceptance of who you are as a person. When you accept yourself you will find that peace and tranquility are much easier to come by in your daily life.

APRIL 27TH: FIRST QUARTER IN LEO

Impressing others and receiving praise will give you a sense of safety and security while the moon is in Leo. This only sets you up for failure, as you'll find yourself at a loss as soon as you're put in the spotlight. The key to navigating through Leo is accepting that feedback and criticism are useful, they help you improve. The first step to accepting these facts is to admit you are afraid of criticism, and to admit that you can't accept criticism. Only once you admit the truth of the problem can you work through it.

RITUAL PLANNER

GOAL/INTENTION:

_____

_____

_____

ITEMS NEEDED:

_____

_____

_____

_____

_____

STEPS:

_____

_____

_____

_____

APRIL HERBS

Elemental gardens are an excellent way to manifest and balance the energies of the four elements. There are a number of ways to call the powers of the elements into your garden. One such way would be to plant herbs associated with each element, such as the herbs in the chart above.

Another method would be for the garden itself to represent Earth, a pinwheel or windchimes for Air, a fountain or rain collection container for Water, and pretty solar lights for Fire. If you have the space, build a path in the shape of a labyrinth into the garden so you may walk the labyrinth meditating upon the four elements.

HERB	SIZE/ SPREAD	START SEEDS INSIDE/OUTSIDE	HARDINESS ZONE	NATIVE REGION	GROWTH TYPE**	SU SO
Chamomile (German)	20-30/ 8-12'	6-8/1-2 before	4-9	US: Northern Colorado to Wisconsin	P	FS/
Heliotrope	1-4'/ 1-2'	NR/4-6 Before Frost	2-11	Eastern Mediterranean Western Asia	P	FS/
Lavender (English)	18-36/ 24"	4-6/Time of Frost	4-9	Southern Europe Asia Minor Australia parts of US	P	FS/
Primrose	6-12"/ 6-18"	6-8/Frost	1-11	Eastern Mediterranean Iran Caucasus	A	FS/

*Weeks before or afer last spring frost

** A=Annual P=Perennial

** FS= full sun, PS= partial sun; WD= well-drained, M= moist, RM, rich moint, L= loamy, LS=loamy/sandy

Properties:
Chamomile: Element- Water. Associated with purification, protection, meditation, and sleep.
Heliotrope: Element- Fire. Named for Greek god of the sun, Helios. The nymph Clytie pined for Helios so deeply she spent all her time sitting and gazing at the sun, not eating or sleeping, so Helios turned her into a flower. She continues to watch the sun from dawn to dusk each day.
Lavender: Element-Air. Considered one of the most valuable herbs that every witch should have.
Primrose: Element- Earth. Often described in folklore as conduit to Otherworld and realm of Faery.

PAUSE & REFLECT

What are some daily rituals that make you happy?

CRYSTALS FOR THE WORKPLACE

The use of crystals is becoming increasingly popular for healing, wellness, and success. I don't just mean by witches, mystics and magi, either. I'm referring to scholars, doctors, corporate leaders, investors, entrepreneurs and more. Crystals have been scientifically proven to have an influence over people and their lives. The electromagnetic field surrounding these crystals have physical, mental, and emotional effects on people. Crystals work psychosomatically as well, as using them in a ritualistic way (i.e. making crystal grid, or taking a break at the same time each day to just hold one in your hand while you space out) triggers certain responses in the brain and body.

It's called the "Piezoelectric effect", a phenomenon in which an electric spark is created when pressure is applied to certain crystals. The term piezoelectricity derives from the Greek words piezo, meaning pressure and electric, meaning amber. French scientist brothers Jacques and Pierre Curie discovered piezoelectricity in 1880, learning that applying pressure to certain crystals created an electric spark.

5 CRYSTALS TO KEEP IN YOUR WORKSPACE

Black Tourmaline: Black Tourmaline is great for grounding, protection, and helping you keep focus, as it helps to block out distractions.

Sodalite: According to DivineTwist, sodalite is the 'Students stone", because it heightens focus, improves clarity, calls in calm, and conjures confidence.

Malachite: This is a personal favorite of mine- I keep my malachite stone right next to my computer. Malachite is great for letting go of hindering behaviors, establishing balance, and promoting growth. It has excellent grounding properties, and inspires creativity.

Green Aventurine: Green aventurine is the stone for people on a mission for money. This is a stone of prosperity; it will help you bring in the cash you need right now (i.e., to pay an unexpected bill), as well as set you up for a steady income growth.

Tigers Eye: I won't even leave the house unless I have either a tumbled stone or my Tiger's eye necklace. This stone cultivates creativity, strengthens willpower, and sharpens your mind.

Final Thoughts

This combination of crystals will aid your writing, work ethic, and your life in general. They are all fairly common stones, so you shouldn't have a difficult time finding them, either as tumbled stones or in raw form. Keep the crystals in a dish or on a mirror and establish a routine where you spend a few moments each day holding one or more stone, mindfully absorbing the energies and applying the effects to your work.

APRIL

	M	T	W	T	F	S	S
13	27	28	29	30	31	1	2
14	3	4	5	6	7	8	9
15	10	11	12	13	14	15	16
16	17	18	19	20	21	22	23
17	24	25	26	27	28	29	30

TO DO LIST

-
-
-
-
-
-
-
-
-

DAILY CARD PULL

Monday

Tuesday

Wednesday

Thursday

Friday

Saturday

Sunday

MONDAY 03

TUESDAY 04
Passover. Begins at Sunset

WEDNESDAY 05

THURSDAY 06 ☽ ♎

2023

FRIDAY	07		GOALS

SATURDAY	08		REMEMBER

-
-
-
-
-
-
-

SUNDAY	09	Easter	NOTES

HABITS	M	T	W	T	F	S	S	NEXT WEEK

APRIL

	M	T	W	T	F	S	S
13	27	28	29	30	31	1	2
14	3	4	5	6	7	8	9
15	10	11	12	13	14	15	16
16	17	18	19	20	21	22	23
17	24	25	26	27	28	29	30

TO DO LIST

-
-
-
-
-
-
-
-
-

DAILY CARD PULL

Monday

Tuesday

Wednesday

Thursday

Friday

Saturday

Sunday

MONDAY 10

TUESDAY 11

WEDNESDAY 12

THURSDAY 13

2023

FRIDAY 14

GOALS

SATURDAY 15

REMEMBER

-
-
-
-
-
-
-
-

SUNDAY 16

NOTES

HABITS

	M	T	W	T	F	S	S

NEXT WEEK

APRIL

	M	T	W	T	F	S	S
13	27	28	29	30	31	1	2
14	3	4	5	6	7	8	9
15	10	11	12	13	14	15	16
16	17	18	19	20	21	22	23
17	24	25	26	27	28	29	30

TO DO LIST

-
-
-
-
-
-
-
-
-

DAILY CARD PULL

Monday

Tuesday

Wednesday

Thursday

Friday

Saturday

Sunday

MONDAY 17

TUESDAY 18

WEDNESDAY 19

THURSDAY 20

2023

FRIDAY	21		GOALS

SATURDAY	22	Earth Day	REMEMBER

-
-
-
-
-
-
-

SUNDAY	23		NOTES

HABITS	M	T	W	T	F	S	S	NEXT WEEK

APRIL

	M	T	W	T	F	S	S
13	27	28	29	30	31	1	2
14	3	4	5	6	7	8	9
15	10	11	12	13	14	15	16
16	17	18	19	20	21	22	23
17	24	25	26	27	28	29	30

TO DO LIST

-
-
-
-
-
-
-
-
-

DAILY CARD PULL

Monday

Tuesday

Wednesday

Thursday

Friday

Saturday

Sunday

MONDAY 24

TUESDAY 25

WEDNESDAY 26

THURSDAY 27

2023

FRIDAY	28		GOALS

SATURDAY 29 ☽ ♌

	REMEMBER
	•
	•
	•
	•
	•
	•
	•

SUNDAY 30

NOTES

HABITS	M	T	W	T	F	S	S	NEXT WEEK

GRATITUDE LIST

_____

_____

_____

_____

_____

_____

_____

MONTHLY TO-DO'S

_____

_____

_____

_____

_____

_____

_____

_____

_____

_____

TRY SOMETHING NEW

CRYSTALS

Crystals work by manipulating energy. A basic understanding of how energy works goes a long way when using crystals in magic. For example, using copper wire to connect a series of crystals in a closed circuit would keep the energy of the crystals cycling in an endless loop, negating the necessity to recharge the crystals with your intention.

CARD SPREAD

Card 1: Who you think you are - Card 2: Who others think you are - Card 3: How to balance the two

SPELL - april fool-me-not spell

Don't let the warmth and light of spring make a fool of you, be objective in your endeavors. Take a small hand mirror, charm it to show you the truth. Mix and powder cinnamon for success, rosemary for clarity of mind, and clove for truth. Sprinkle over the mirror, then wash clean with water. Use mirror for scrying to divine about important decisions, especially regarding career and relationships.

ENTITY

House guardians can be powerful and effective in protecting your home and those who live within. Study various methods of creating/connecting with house guardians and consider exploring this technique.

SELF-CARE

Digital spring cleaning! Empty your voicemails, delete those 5,000 emails, trash the duplicate photos, along with accidental photos looking up your nose and taken from inside your pocket. Organize your desktop/computer, delete apps you haven't used. Your electronics will thank you!

TEA

There is another kind of tea that we drink that isn't actually tea, but an herbal infusion- steeping parts of an herb or a collection of herbs in hot water. Herbal infusions don't necessarily have to be steeped in hot water – combining water and herbs in a glass container that is left in the sun will result in an infusion as well, albeit a much milder, subtler flavor than that which was exposed to high temperatures.

HERBS

Buckeye is the Gambler's herb, for its' strong ability for good luck, wealth, and prosperity. The buckeye tree is native to midwestern U.S., and the nuts, although toxic to humans when consumed, can be dried and carried in a sachet to attract money and wealth. If the buckeye tree doesn't grow near you, you can bake candy buckeye's, made of chocolate and peanut butter, infused with intentions of good luck, prosperity, and success.

Record a Card Pull

DECK USED:

_____

CARD(S) PULLED:

_____

_____

_____

YOUR INTERPRETATION:

_____

_____

_____

_____

_____

_____

BOOK INTERPRETATION:

_____

_____

_____

_____

_____

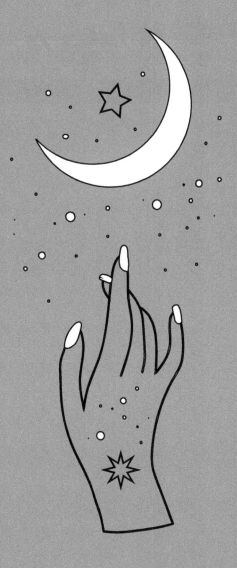

"As an artist, if your work doesn't inflame at least part of the audience, then you might as well call it quits and sell insurance... The world needs more boundary pushers, not more boundary creators."

- Alys Arden

May

Calendar Key
 Full Moon   First Quarter   Eclipse
 New Moon   Last Quarter   Sun

APRIL

M	T	W	T	F	S	S
					1	2
3	4	5	6	7	8	9
10	11	12	13	14	15	16
17	18	19	20	21	22	23
24	25	26	27	28	29	30

JUNE

M	T	W	T	F	S	S
		1	2	3	4	
5	6	7	8	9	10	11
12	13	14	15	16	17	18
19	20	21	22	23	24	25
26	27	28	29	30		

Goals

Notes

_____
_____
_____
_____
_____
_____
_____
_____
_____
_____
_____
_____

Monday	Tuesday	Wednesday
1 121/244 Beltane	**2** 122/243	**3** 123/242
8 128/237	**9** 129/236	**10** 130/235
15 135/230	**16** 136/229	**17** 137/228
22 142/223	**23** 143/222	**24** 144/221
29 149/216 Memorial Day	**30** 150/215	**31** 151/214

MAY

M	T	W	T	F	S	S
1	2	3	4	5	6	7
8	9	10	11	12	13	14
15	16	17	18	19	20	21
22	23	24	25	26	27	28
29	30	31				

Thursday	Friday	Saturday	Sunday
4 124/241	5 125/240 ♏	6 126/239	7 127/238
1 131/234	12 132/233 ♒	13 133/232	14 134/231 Mother's Day
8 138/227	19 139/226 ● ♉	20 140/225	21 141/224 ☼ ♊
5 145/220	26 146/219	27 147/218 ♍	28 148/217

LUNAR PHASES

MAY 5TH: FULL MOON IN SCORPIO

The full moon in Scorpio provides powerful energy for emotional healing and exploration. It's a time to really step back and examine your life, especially your relationships, to determine what could be holding you back, and what could bring you ahead. This moon will provide the courage and clarity needed for communicating with loved ones in order to strengthen relationships.

MAY 12TH: LAST QUARTER IN AQUARIUS

The moon in Aquarius gives us the need for emotional freedoms which can cause complications in our relationships. Can also be a time when you are able to better understand your emotions, freeing you from negative feelings such as jealousy, fear, and anger.

MAY 19TH: NEW MOON IN TAURUS

Your sense of safety arises from the need for stability which is difficult to find at the moment. The key to stability is acceptance – accepting that change is a part of life, and acceptance of who you are as a person. When you accept yourself you will find that peace and tranquility are much easier to come by in your daily life.

MAY 27TH: FIRST QUARTER IN VIRGO

The Virgo moon is one of order and practicality. You feel you have to reorganize and bring order to anything you feel is in chaos. This can lead to being intolerant of others, so try focusing more on solving problems, creating order within your life, and helping others without judgement.

RITUAL PLANNER

GOAL/INTENTION:

_____

_____

_____

ITEMS NEEDED:

_____

_____

_____

_____

_____

STEPS:

_____

_____

_____

_____

MAY HERB PLANTING GUIDE: FAERY GARDENS

The intention behind creating a Faery garden is typically to honor or acknowledge the Fae, to invite them into your life, or a combination of the two. Fae can be powerful magical allies, especially when it comes to gardening. When I planted my first garden I had no clue what I was doing. I knew the basics, but I didn't have the touch. My plants were weak and withering. It was quite heartbreaking to see these plants I had brought to life drom a mere seed struggling for their lives. That's when I decided to reach out to the Good Neighbors (always use euphemisms when you're communicating with the Fae, as calling them faery is offensive). I started turning my pathetic flower and herb garden into a Faery garden.

I purchased fairy statues from the dollar store, made little signs that said things like "Welcome" and "Bright Blessings" that I stuck around the plants of the garden. In the front and middle space of the garden I placed a large, flat stone I found in the woods. With acrylic paint I painted a seven-point star, the faery star, on the rock and glued plastic gems at each point. I announced that I would be sporadically leaving offerings as a sign of respect for the Good Neighbors on the land – never promise to leave offerings on a regular basis unless you're 100% positive you can carry out that promise- and that's just what I did. I usually put a little cup of milk with honey, and sometimes a piece of my morning toast, or a cookie from that evenings' dessert.

There'd be times I'd see something in my home, like an old piece of jewelry or a little knickknack and I'd get the geeling that I should give it to the Fae, so I would. After about a month of this i felt I had gained their trust, so I prepared a really special offering of sweets, milk and honey, handmade gifts, and I brought them out at sunset. I laid them on the stone and turned towards the woods where the clan resided. I greeted them warmly, expressed my gratitude for them letting me live on their land, and finally asked them to help me with the garden.

In exchange I promised to keep planting the garden every spring, and to leave them offerings whenever I thought of it.

That garden went from weed-ridden, drooping and frail to lush with life. Flowers were vivid shades of all colors, many growing taller than me. The weeds that had once threatened to choke the life out of my plants were totally gone 2 weeks later – I never pulled any up, never put down any weed killer, never even used mulch. They just thinned out and stopped growing. I didn't have to water the garden either – it seemed to rain just when the soil started to dry out. I kept the flowers pruned, deadheading, cutting, and such, duties that allowed me to touch each flower, familiarizing myself with its' spirit.

HYDROMANDY

by Kiki Dombrowski

There are many of ways to use water for divination, and this article will look at some of the ways you can use water divination in your life.

Scrying is the art of the gaze. People commonly associate scrying with gazing into a crystal ball or dark mirror. However, all you need to scry is a reflective surface, and the surface of water is a very organic and peaceful place to practice this form of divination. If you want to try water scrying indoors find a wide and shallow bowl, preferably a darker bowl. Fill it with water, and if you'd like to make it even darker, add a few drops of black ink. Place the bowl on a table and put two small candles on both sides of the bowl. Dim or turn off the lights and move around the candles, so you see a gentle glow from the candles in the bowl. You want to be able to look into the surface and not see a direct or clear reflection of the flame, just a glow of light. Gaze into the water when you are ready: it will feel almost like you are staring through the water, or your vision might go hazy. Keep your sessions to a few minutes at first, and as you become more comfortable, you can lengthen your sessions.

OBJECTS IN WATER

An ancient method of hydromancy requires a ring on a string or a pendulum and a jar with water. Lower the ring or pendulum into the water and shake the jar. The number

of times the ring or pendulum hits the sides of
the jar can help predict the future. One way to consider
interpreting this is if it hits the jar an even number of
times the answer is "yes." If it hits the jar an odd number of
times, the answer is "no." If it doesn't hit the side of
the jar, then ask again later. If it hits the side of the jar only a
few times or slowly, the outcome will be slow to
reveal itself. If it hits the side of the jar frequently or quickly,
the outcome will be immediate.

Another ancient method of hydromancy involves throwing
pebbles into the water and studying the ripples and
sounds the water makes after the object is in the water. If you
want to try this, throw a pebble into a body of
water and watch the ripples come from it. Do they expand far
out? Perhaps the further out the ripples expand,
the more optimistic the reading is. Do you see a certain
number of rings? This may be an indication of time or
amount.

LECANOMANCY
 Lecanomancy is the divination of oil on water. Take a bowl of
warm water and pour a small amount
(maybe a teaspoon) of oil onto the top of the water. Read the
shapes that the oil makes in the water. If there is
an unbroken ring of oil the answer is positive. If the oil covers
the entire surface, the answer is negative. Small
droplets of oil can signify money. If there are two divided
sections of oil, there may be turmoil or drama ahead!

OCEAN DIVINATION
 If you are fortunate enough to live by the ocean, consider
using the water and the sand for divination. You
may want to try and search for different shells or patterns in
the sand and interpret that. Or, you can watch the
water, perhaps ask a question, and see how the waves respond
to your question.

PAUSE & REFLECT

If you could live as someone else for a week, who would it be and
why?

MAY FESTIVALS

During the months of April and May, the people of Vanuatu on Pentecost Island perform the Ritual of Naghol, either as a coming-of-age ceremony or to bless the earth for a bountiful yam harvest. The main event of this ritual is land-diving. About 30 men take turns leaping from 75-foot wooden towers. The only thing keeping these men from crashing to their deaths is a vine tied to their ankle. It was this ritual that inspired Bungee Jumping. Dramas and songs are performed before the jump, and the ritual is brough to a close by feasting.
[Source: https://www.mentalfloss.com/article/19055/early-history-bungee-jumping]

USE THE SPACE BELOW TO RECORD YOUR MAY CELEBRATIONS

MAY

	M	T	W	T	F	S	S
18	1	2	3	4	5	6	7
19	8	9	10	11	12	13	14
20	15	16	17	18	19	20	21
21	22	23	24	25	26	27	28
22	29	30	31	1	2	3	4

TO DO LIST

-
-
-
-
-
-
-
-
-

DAILY CARD PULL

Monday

Tuesday

Wednesday

Thursday

Friday

Saturday

Sunday

MONDAY | 01 | Beltane

TUESDAY | 02

WEDNESDAY | 03

THURSDAY | 04

2023

FRIDAY 05 ☾ ♏

GOALS

SATURDAY 06

REMEMBER

-
-
-
-
-
-
-

SUNDAY 07

NOTES

HABITS

	M	T	W	T	F	S	S

NEXT WEEK

MAY

	M	T	W	T	F	S	S
18	1	2	3	4	5	6	7
19	8	9	10	11	12	13	14
20	15	16	17	18	19	20	21
21	22	23	24	25	26	27	28
22	29	30	31	1	2	3	4

TO DO LIST

-
-
-
-
-
-
-
-
-

DAILY CARD PULL

Monday

Tuesday

Wednesday

Thursday

Friday

Saturday

Sunday

MONDAY 08

TUESDAY 09

WEDNESDAY 10

THURSDAY 11

2023

FRIDAY	12 🌓 ≈		GOALS
• Ritual for emotional clarity			

SATURDAY	13		REMEMBER
			•
•
•
•
•
•
•

SUNDAY	14	Mother's Day	NOTES

HABITS	M	T	W	T	F	S	S	NEXT WEEK

MAY

	M	T	W	T	F	S	S
18	1	2	3	4	5	6	7
19	8	9	10	11	12	13	14
20	15	16	17	18	19	20	21
21	22	23	24	25	26	27	28
22	29	30	31	1	2	3	4

TO DO LIST

-
-
-
-
-
-
-
-
-

DAILY CARD PULL

Monday

Tuesday

Wednesday

Thursday

Friday

Saturday

Sunday

MONDAY	15

TUESDAY	16

WEDNESDAY	17

THURSDAY	18

2023

FRIDAY	19 ● ♉		GOALS

SATURDAY	20		REMEMBER

REMEMBER
-
-
-
-
-
-
-
-

SUNDAY	21 ☀ ♊		NOTES

HABITS	M	T	W	T	F	S	S	NEXT WEEK

MAY

	M	T	W	T	F	S	S
18	1	2	3	4	5	6	7
19	8	9	10	11	12	13	14
20	15	16	17	18	19	20	21
21	22	23	24	25	26	27	28
22	29	30	31	1	2	3	4

TO DO LIST

-
-
-
-
-
-
-
-
-

DAILY CARD PULL

Monday

Tuesday

Wednesday

Thursday

Friday

Saturday

Sunday

MONDAY 22

TUESDAY 23

WEDNESDAY 24

THURSDAY 25

2023

FRIDAY	26		GOALS

SATURDAY	27 ◑ ♍		REMEMBER

REMEMBER
-
-
-
-
-
-
-

SUNDAY	28		NOTES

HABITS	M	T	W	T	F	S	S	NEXT WEEK

JUNE

	M	T	W	T	F	S	S
22	29	30	31	1	2	3	4
23	5	6	7	8	9	10	11
24	12	13	14	15	16	17	18
25	19	20	21	22	23	24	25
26	26	27	28	29	30	1	2

TO DO LIST

-
-
-
-
-
-
-
-
-

DAILY CARD PULL

Monday

Tuesday

Wednesday

Thursday

Friday

Saturday

Sunday

MONDAY	29	Memorial Day

TUESDAY	30	

WEDNESDAY	31	

THURSDAY	01	

2023

FRIDAY	02		GOALS

SATURDAY	03		REMEMBER

REMEMBER
-
-
-
-
-
-
-

SUNDAY	04	☾⚔	NOTES

HABITS	M	T	W	T	F	S	S	NEXT WEEK

GRATITUDE LIST

_____

_____

_____

_____

_____

_____

_____

MONTHLY TO-DO'S

_____

_____

_____

_____

_____

_____

_____

_____

_____

_____

TRY SOMETHING NEW

CRYSTALS
Lapis Lazuli, known for its' vivid blue color, has been used by the ancients as eyeshadow, protective amulets, love potions, antidotes to poison, and to enhance psychic abilities. Modern practitioners have zeroed in on the magic of this crystal, realizing its ability to work on a psychic and spiritual level. It's uses today are to enhance psychic ability, strengthen intuition, find one's soul mate, and as means of protection of the body, mind, and soul.

CARD SPREAD
Card 1: Sexual empowerment - Card 2: Magical empowerment - Card 3: Spiritual empowerment.

SPELL Glamour for Greatness spell. Glamour magic is a technique that makes qualities of your choosing prominent to others – so you are perceived how you wish to be perceived. Whether it's greatness in work, life, love, or other, glamour is how you'll achieve it.

ENTITY
Using a deity dictionary – either digital or a printed book – and pick a spirit at random. Learn all you can about this entity, exploring the various cultures who influenced it Who knows, maybe they're meant to be in your life?

SELF-CARE
It's that time of year – spring cleaning. It's so worth it though. If you need to break it down and take it one room at a time – hell, take one section of one room at a time if you must, so long as you get it done before summer starts.

TEA:
Enhance the efficacy of your tea magic by crafting a tea specifically suited to your intention. Choose a combination of herbs/plants with specific properties that will meet your needs, which you will then steep in water to create your unique magical tea. When designing your recipe, there are a few things to consider that can help: flavor (sweet vs. savory, strong vs. subtle); source (purchase, plant, harvest); shelf life; additives; intended use (ingest, topical, energy/spiritual consumption, practical and/or household use). I do recommend, once you decide on your ingredients, you research your choices thoroughly to ensure you have nothing but an enlightening, exciting, enriching experience.

HERBS
Herbs may be used a number of ways in magic. They can be dried and crushed, to dress a candle or make incense. They can be added to spell jars, and stems may be woven into wreathes. They can even be grown inside in a pot or outside in a garden, allowing the magic of the live plant to alter the energies of the home inside or out.

Record a Card Pull

DECK USED:

_____

CARD(S) PULLED:

_____

_____

_____

YOUR INTERPRETATION:

_____

_____

_____

_____

_____

_____

BOOK INTERPRETATION:

_____

_____

_____

_____

_____

"You will never be enough for everyone. Ever. You will never please enough people, appease enough people, you will never fulfill everything for everyone. So... fuck it. Write for you. Paint for you. Craft for you. Do it for you, because you're the only one worth the effort to please, because it will never be everyone."

- Tonya Brown

June

Calendar Key
- Full Moon
- New Moon
- First Quarter
- Last Quarter
- Eclipse
- Sun

MAY

M	T	W	T	F	S	S
1	2	3	4	5	6	7
8	9	10	11	12	13	14
15	16	17	18	19	20	21
22	23	24	25	26	27	28
29	30	31				

JULY

M	T	W	T	F	S	S
					1	2
3	4	5	6	7	8	9
10	11	12	13	14	15	16
17	18	19	20	21	22	23
24	25	26	27	28	29	30

Goals

Notes

Monday	Tuesday	Wednesday
5 156/209	**6** 157/208	**7** 158/207
12 163/202	**13** 164/201	**14** 165/200
19 170/195	**20** 171/194	**21** 172/193 Summer Solstice
26 177/188 ♎	**27** 178/187	**28** 179/186

JUNE

M	T	W	T	F	S	S
			1	2	3	4
5	6	7	8	9	10	11
12	13	14	15	16	17	18
19	20	21	22	23	24	25
26	27	28	29	30		

Thursday	Friday	Saturday	Sunday
152/213	2 153/212	3 154/211	4 155/210 ♐
159/206	9 160/205	10 161/204 ♓	11 162/203
166/199	16 167/198 Juneteenth	17 168/197	18 169/196 Father's Day ♋
173/192	23 174/191	24 175/190	25 176/189
180/185	30 181/184		

GOALS & DREAMS

6-MONTH PROJECT LIST

GOAL: _____ DUE DATE: _____

ENVISION YOUR LIFE AFTER OBTAINING YOUR GOAL.
HOW DO YOU FEEL?

_____

_____

_____

_____

_____

MONTHLY ACTION STEPS:

_____

_____

_____

_____

_____

NOTES:

_____

_____

_____

_____

LUNAR PHASES

JUNE 4TH: FULL MOON IN SAGITTARIUS

The moon in Sagittarius is the most optimistic of energies, giving you a craving for new experiences and adventure. Motivations under the Sagittarius moon are driven by the need for the truth, or finding something, be it a philosophy, a goal or new hobby. You may be inclined to overdo things, so make sure you don't forget to count your blessings and appreciate what you have right now.

JUNE 10TH: LAST QUARTER IN PISCES

Pisces moon generates an energy that helps you define your feelings and connecting with your dreams. The last quarter moon will influence this energy so that it is particularly helpful when it comes to resolving issues, bringing projects to a close, and re-examining pursuits that are not going to suit your needs or work out the way you had hoped.

JUNE 18TH: NEW MOON IN CANCER

The Moon in Cancer instills in you emotional security and a sense of belonging, a sense of nurturing you feel instinctively. You find that you're longing for an intimate connection that's meaningful and long-lasting, enough so you can establish a sense of belonging- put down roots, a place to bunker down as the Universe throws its' trials and tribulations at you. Using the Full Moon energies to work a self-love spell may help to satisfy this desire.

JUNE 26TH: FIRST QUARTER IN LIBRA

The moon in Libra drives us for a sense of order, but unlike that of the moon in Virgo, we are satisfied by pleasant interactions and aesthetics in the environment. The need for order and harmony are strong, and rather than deal with confrontation you try to keep everything 'nice'. Don't let the Libra moon make you forget who you are, and certainly resist the urge to bottle up your feelings.

RITUAL PLANNER

GOAL/INTENTION:

_____

_____

_____

ITEMS NEEDED:

_____

_____

_____

_____

_____

STEPS:

_____

_____

_____

_____

JUNE HERB GUIDE

Bees and Butterflies are environmentally vital, beneficial to our gardens, and make excellent magical allies. Bees are amazing communicators, highly productive, possess incredible endurance and determination, and are natures collectors. Channeling the Bee can aid you in the collection of wisdom, instill endurance and determination in the pursuit of your goals, and help you learn to communicate clearly and effectively. Butterflies are symbols of transformation, and can even aid in spiritual shapeshifting, as they transition from a worm-like caterpillar to the delicate, beautiful butterfly.

HERB	SIZE/ SPREAD	START SEEDS INSIDE/OUTSIDE	HARDINESS ZONE	NATIVE REGION	GROWTH TYPE**	SUN/- SOIL**
nise vssop	2-4'/1.5-3'	Direct Sow in Fall	4-9	Europe, North Africa, some parts of Asia	A	FS/WD
)ill	2-4'/2-3'	10-12/ NR – seed needs soil	9-11	Peru	P	FS/RL
nnel	4-6'/18-36"	8-12/ 1-2 before	5-8	Mediterranean Region	P	FS/WD
mmer vory	12-18"/3'	NR/ after frost	4-9	North America	P	FS/M,W D

'eeks before or afer last spring frost

A=Annual P=Perennial

FS= full sun, PS= partial sun; WD= well-drained, M= moist, RM, rich moint, L= loamy, LS=loamy/sandy

Magic Properties:
Anise Hyssop: Protection, Purification, Cleansing, Blessings
Dill: Love Spells, Dispel Bad Dreams and Jealousy, Emotional Balance
Fennel: Courage, Strength, Protection, Love/Fertility, Divination
Summer Savory: Enhance Sex Life ,Improve Concentration and Memory, Empowerment

Record a Card Pull

DECK USED:

_____

CARD(S) PULLED:

_____

_____

_____

YOUR INTERPRETATION:

_____

_____

_____

_____

_____

_____

BOOK INTERPRETATION:

_____

_____

_____

_____

_____

_____

DIY HERBAL STICKS
by Kiki Dombrowski

Herbal Sticks are a bundle of dried herbs wrapped tightly together with string. The tip of the stick is lit and the smoke from the bundle of herbs is used to purify and cleanse the energy of an area or a person.

HOW TO MAKE YOUR OWN

1. You will need herbs, cotton string, and scissors.

2. Collect the herbs and flowers you wish to use. Only pick what you need, and do not pick anything that is rare, may have pesticides on it, or that you do not have permission to harvest. Some common herbs and flowers you may want to consider using are garden sage, rosemary, lavender, sweet grass, and cedar leaves.

3. Decide the size of the stick you want. If you want larger sticks, make sure that there is enough stem and the plants you collect are between seven and ten inches. You can also make smaller ones that are only between three and five inches.

4. Clean and arrange the plants. Make sure that all the stems are at facing downwards and the flowers/ tops of the plants are facing upwards.

5. Gather all the ingredients together at the bottoms of the stick and tie it together with a strong knot. This is the base of the stick, so use a lot of string to wrap this tightly.

6. Slowly start to wrap the string from the base upwards towards the tip of the stick. Make sure that you wrap them tightly. When you reach the top area where you want to stop, start wrapping the string back down towards the base of the stick. When you get to the bottom tie the string off with another strong knot.

7. Hang the sticks to dry. I like to hang them to air dry in front of a window. You can also dry them on a rack. It will take at least a week for the bundles to dry out completely, depending on the size of the stick.

PAUSE & REFLECT

Do you plan to pass on your magic or traditions? If so, to who?

_____

_____

_____

_____

_____

_____

_____

_____

_____

_____

_____

_____

_____

_____

_____

JUNE FESTIVALS

June is known as Pride Month in the United States. Three important events in the gay liberation movement took place in June. The first being the Stonewall Riots on June 29th, 1969, which was a series of demonstrations by the LGBTQIA+ community and their supporters in response to the police raids on the Stonewall Inn in Greenwich Village, NY on June 28th.

June 28th, 1970 marks the date of the first gay pride marches which were carried out simultaneously in New York, Los Angeles, and San Francisco.

On June 26, 2015, the U.S. Supreme Court struck down all state bans on same-sex marriage, legalized it in all fifty states.

[Source: https://youth.gov/feature-article/june-lgbt-pride-month]

USE THE SPACE BELOW TO RECORD YOUR JUNE CELEBRATIONS

JUNE

	M	T	W	T	F	S	S
22	29	30	31	1	2	3	4
23	5	6	7	8	9	10	11
24	12	13	14	15	16	17	18
25	19	20	21	22	23	24	25
26	26	27	28	29	30	1	2

TO DO LIST

-
-
-
-
-
-
-
-
-

DAILY CARD PULL

Monday

Tuesday

Wednesday

Thursday

Friday

Saturday

Sunday

MONDAY 05

TUESDAY 06

WEDNESDAY 07

THURSDAY 08

2023

FRIDAY	09		GOALS

SATURDAY	10	☽ ♓	REMEMBER

REMEMBER
- •
- •
- •
- •
- •
- •
- •

SUNDAY	11		NOTES

HABITS		M	T	W	T	F	S	S	NEXT WEEK

JUNE

	M	T	W	T	F	S	S
22	29	30	31	1	2	3	4
23	5	6	7	8	9	10	11
24	12	13	14	15	16	17	18
25	19	20	21	22	23	24	25
26	26	27	28	29	30	1	2

TO DO LIST

-
-
-
-
-
-
-
-
-

DAILY CARD PULL

Monday

Tuesday

Wednesday

Thursday

Friday

Saturday

Sunday

MONDAY 12

TUESDAY 13

WEDNESDAY 14

THURSDAY 15

2023

FRIDAY	16	Juneteenth

GOALS

SATURDAY	17	

REMEMBER

-
-
-
-
-
-
-

SUNDAY	18	Father's Day

NOTES

HABITS

	M	T	W	T	F	S	S

NEXT WEEK

JUNE

	M	T	W	T	F	S	S
22	29	30	31	1	2	3	4
23	5	6	7	8	9	10	11
24	12	13	14	15	16	17	18
25	19	20	21	22	23	24	25
26	26	27	28	29	30	1	2

TO DO LIST

-
-
-
-
-
-
-
-
-

DAILY CARD PULL

- Monday
- Tuesday
- Wednesday
- Thursday
- Friday
- Saturday
- Sunday

MONDAY | 19

TUESDAY | 20

WEDNESDAY | 21 Summer Solstice

THURSDAY | 22

2023

FRIDAY	23	

GOALS

SATURDAY	24	

REMEMBER

-
-
-
-
-
-
-

SUNDAY	25	

NOTES

HABITS

	M	T	W	T	F	S	S

NEXT WEEK

JUNE

	M	T	W	T	F	S	S
22	29	30	31	1	2	3	4
23	5	6	7	8	9	10	11
24	12	13	14	15	16	17	18
25	19	20	21	22	23	24	25
26	26	27	28	29	30	1	2

TO DO LIST

-
-
-
-
-
-
-
-
-

DAILY CARD PULL

Monday

Tuesday

Wednesday

Thursday

Friday

Saturday

Sunday

MONDAY 26 ◐ Ω

TUESDAY 27

WEDNESDAY 28

THURSDAY 29

2023

FRIDAY	30	

GOALS

SATURDAY	01	

REMEMBER

-
-
-
-
-
-
-

SUNDAY	02	

NOTES

HABITS	M	T	W	T	F	S	S

NEXT WEEK

GRATITUDE LIST

_____
_____
_____
_____
_____
_____
_____

MONTHLY TO-DO'S

_____
_____
_____
_____
_____
_____
_____
_____
_____
_____

TRY SOMETHING NEW

CRYSTALS

Crystals all have a variety of uses, but it's important to properly care for your crystal in order to maintain maximum efficiency. For each intention, a crystal should be cleared of energies that have built up within and around the stone, and then charged anew with the next intention. To clear the crystal, you may use sunlight, moonlight, running water, crystals with cleansing properties, or your will. Each crystal is unique, so be sure to do some research to ensure that the method you choose will not have harmful effects on the stone (i.e., some stones dissolve in water, fade in sunlight). The two methods I have found to pose little to no risk to any gem is that of moonlight and personal will power. To charge your crystal, hold the stone in your dominant hand, declare your intent or objective, and send that declaration into the stone via visualization.

CARD SPREAD

Card 1: Miss it - Card 2: Make it - Card 3: Mean it

SPELL

Longevity spell. Take 9 strands of string. work into 3 braids, with 3 strands each, then braid the three braids together. While your weaving and working, envision what it is you wish to keep going strong and true – your career, a project, creative streak. Once the three braids have been braided together as one, tie the ends together, so the braid is in a circle, a symbol of eternity, and keeps the energy cycling around and around. .

ENTITY

Make an altar for house spirits/the spirit of the home. Hearths are few and far between nowadays, so set it up somewhere in the home where your family congregates often – in the living room, by the kitchen stove, near the dining table.

SELF-CARE

Write a "Thank You" letter to yourself. Be sure to extend gratitude for your hard work, your sacrifices, your beauty and your talents.

TEA:

Now the summer is here, and the temperatures are heating up, why not heat up your life a bit and try different flavors of green tea, as green tea is known for exciting your passions, be they sexual, spiritual, home life, or work life.

HERBS

Clover is often associated with good luck and prosperity but has been known to be used to ward off evil spirits and strengthen psychic abilities in some Scandinavian countries. Hanging a bundle of clover over your front door will keep malicious beings, human or otherwise, at bay, allowing only energies of luck and fortune through the threshold. Carry a sachet of dried clover with you to a job interview or stick some in your pocket when you gamble.

Record a Card Pull

DECK USED:

_____

CARD(S) PULLED:

_____

_____

_____

YOUR INTERPRETATION:

_____

_____

_____

_____

_____

_____

BOOK INTERPRETATION:

_____

_____

_____

_____

_____

_____

"You do it because the doing of it is the thing. The doing is the thing. The talking and worrying and thinking is not the thing."

- Amy Poehler

July

Calendar Key
- 🌑 Full Moon
- ⚫ New Moon
- 🌓 First Quarter
- 🌗 Last Quarter
- 🌘 Eclipse
- ☀ Sun

JUNE

M	T	W	T	F	S	S
			1	2	3	4
5	6	7	8	9	10	11
12	13	14	15	16	17	18
19	20	21	22	23	24	25
26	27	28	29	30		

AUGUST

M	T	W	T	F	S	S
1	2	3	4	5	6	
7	8	9	10	11	12	13
14	15	16	17	18	19	20
21	22	23	24	25	26	27
28	29	30	31			

Goals

Notes

_____
_____
_____
_____
_____
_____
_____
_____
_____
_____
_____

	Monday	Tuesday	Wednesday
31	212/153		
3	184/181 🌑♑	4	185/180 Independence Day	5	186/179
10	191/174 🌓♈	11	192/173	12	193/172
17	198/167 ⚫♋	18	199/166	19	200/165
24	205/160	25	206/159 🌓♎	26	207/158

JULY

M	T	W	T	F	S	S
31					1	2
3	4	5	6	7	8	9
10	11	12	13	14	15	16
17	18	19	20	21	22	23
24	25	26	27	28	29	30

Thursday	Friday	Saturday	Sunday
		1 182/183	2 183/182
6 187/178	7 188/177	8 189/176	9 190/175
13 194/171	14 195/170 Bastille Day	15 196/169	16 197/168
20 201/164	21 202/163	22 203/162	23 204/161 ☀♌
27 208/157	28 209/156	29 210/155	30 211/154

LUNAR PHASES

JULY 3RD: FULL MOON IN CAPRICORN

The moon in Capricorn has an emotional seriousness, a sober orientation, and a practical awareness that brings with it a need to feel useful. Using the energies of the new moon and amplified ambitions of Capricorn, this is an ideal time to start new projects.

JULY 10TH: LAST QUARTER IN ARIES

The moon in Aries is emotionally direct and impulsive, with strong, influential feelings. Time for a fresh start, learning new behaviors, establishing new habits. Just don't rush to make decisions, as Aries is apt to do, feeling as though quicker is better. It's not. Take your time to consider what you need, what you want, and choose carefully. The choices made in Aries set the tone for the extended future.

JULY 17TH: NEW MOON IN CANCER

The Moon in Cancer instills in you emotional security and a sense of belonging, a sense of nurturing you feel instinctively. You find that you're longing for an intimate connection that's meaningful and long-lasting, enough so you can establish a sense of belonging- put down roots, a place to bunker down as the Universe throws its' trials and tribulations at you. Using the Full Moon energies to work a self-love spell may help to satisfy this desire.

JULY 25TH: FIRST QUARTER IN SCORPIO

Scorpio energy encourages us to explore our feelings more deeply, and we find we're drawn to sex, power and money. Learning what gets other people going is arousing. Instinctive orientation is to start over from scratch. Only by destroying the roots of disturbances can you begin healing.

RITUAL PLANNER

GOAL/INTENTION:

_____

_____

_____

ITEMS NEEDED:

_____

_____

_____

_____

_____

STEPS:

_____

_____

_____

_____

JULY FESTIVALS

The Festival of San Fermin, locally known as Sanfermines, is a week-long festival celebrated in Spain to honor the first Spanish bishop, Saint Fermin. While the festival is best known for the Running of the Bulls, there are a number of other traditional and folkloric events that take place at the Festival of San Fermin. The festival commences by setting off a firework, the "chupinazo", a rocket launched at noon on July 6th from a city hall balcony while thousands of people celebrate in the city hall square.

July 7th features the Saint Fermin procession, an event in which thousands of people accompany the 15th century statue of Saint Fermin through the old section of Pamplona. The procession is joined by street performers, dancers, and the emergence of 'gigantes', gigantic wood-framed-paper-mâché puppets controlled from the inside, which dance and twirl down the street when the cathedral bell "Maria" starts to ring. The festival ends at midnight of July 14th, with everyone gathered in the candle-lit city square singing Pobre de mí.

[Source: https://en.wikipedia.org/wiki/FestivaloßanFerm%C3%ADn]

JULY HERBAL PLANTING GUIDE: GARDENING METHODS

Once you decide on what you want to plant, you'll have to decide how you'll plant them – the gardening method. The most common gardening methods are in-ground, raised row, raised bed, and container, and there are benefits and drawbacks to each method.

In-Ground Gardening

In-ground gardens are just as they sound- you'll dig up the grass, pull out rocks and weeds, add nutrient rich soil and plant directly into the ground. While this is the most affordable method of gardening, it requires the most time and effort to create and maintain.

Raised Row Gardening

Raised Row gardens are in-ground gardens with raised areas of soil and organic material (i.e. compost, shredded leaves, mulch, straw) formed into rows or hills. The goal of a raised row garden is to build mounds of rich, healthy soil that continually breaks down, improving the entire garden space. Building the mounds will take some time and effort, and high quality soil can be fairly expensive, but maintenance of the garden is minimal because you won't have to weed and pests are less likely to be an issue, and you'll have a higher yield and longer growing time because the higher mounds allow for a deeper, stronger root system.

Raised Bed Gardening

A raised garden bed is a bottomless container, made of either wood, plastic, stone, or concrete, filled with high-quality soil that sits on top of the ground. The raised bed could be purchased, custom built, or you could build it yourself. Pick a sunny part of your lawn to put the bed and fill it about a quarter of the way with organic matter (i.e. compost), then fill it up to about 2" below the top of the frame with mid to high-quality soil. As the organic matter breaks down it will enhance the soil, and allowing for deep and strong root systems which will prevent weed growth. To deter pests either cover the bed with a screen or tent or plant pest-deterring plants.

Container Gardening

A container garden is one that grows in a container. If the container can hold soil, then you can use it to hold a garden- so long as you can drill holes in the bottom to allow for drainage (not applicable to grow bags because they are not watertight). Some possible containers you could use are traditional pots, boxes, bins, grow bags, barrels, troughs, tubs – even a tin can. This method is ideal for people who don't have a yard or space to put down a garden, are unable or don't wish to spend a great deal of time outside or participating in a physically exerting activity.

One of the major benefits to this method is that you have control over the growing conditions. This method could be expensive but there are ways to cut costs without depriving the plants, such as using a container you have in your home instead of buying a new plant pot.

SMOKELESS CLEANSING

by Briony Silver

The anticipation felt before beginning a well-planned ritual is nearly universal in the magical community. You may have spent days, weeks, or even months gathering your materials, writing your own incantations, physically preparing the area, and meticulously planning out every step. As the time arrives, you might begin by energetically cleansing your home—perhaps reaching for your go-to herb bundle, setting it ablaze, and moving it intentionally around the space while watching tendrils of smoke drift through the air.

It is often at this point that people start to really transition into that "ritual headspace," as our sense of smell is tremendously powerful. But what happens when that oh-so-common magical mishap strikes and the next sound you hear is not your carefully curated spell work soundtrack, but instead the piercing shriek of your smoke detector? It's enough to jolt anyone sharply back into a mundane mindset as you sprint to open windows, turn on fans, and clear the air as quickly as possible. And after such a startling interruption, it can sometimes be a challenge to pick up where you left off.

There are a number of reasons it may be beneficial to have some smoke-free cleansing methods in your witchy toolkit, the scenario above being just one of them. You or a member of your household might be sensitive to smoke, perhaps you're working in a space that prohibits burning of any kind, or maybe you just don't like the smell of burning herbs. Whatever the reason, if fire is not an option for your cleansing activities, consider looking to its opposite element— water—for an inspiring alternative: asperging.

Simply put, asperging is the act of ritually scattering or sprinkling water around a space (or onto an object) to energetically cleanse it. One of the beautiful things about this technique is that it is so highly customizable. Below are just a few different ways that you can make it your own:

Water: If you already have some sacred water on hand, great! If not, it can be relatively simple to create your own. Plain filtered water can provide a solid foundation, or feel free to use any other natural water you have available. Sea water can be a particularly well-suited option, as it combines both water and salt.

Ingredients: This is where crafting your sacred water can get really fun! If you're not using sea water, salt is an excellent first ingredient. You can use sea salt, pink salt, black salt, plain table salt, or any combination thereof. Just be careful when using black salt. If too much is used, it can darken the water and potentially stain any light surfaces onto which the droplets fall. You may also add some herbs, oils, or crystals to your potion. It's important to exercise caution if adding crystals, though, as not all crystals are water-safe and some can be damaged by salt. When in doubt, the indirect method of charging (placing the stones in a glass bowl or container within the water, ensuring there is no direct contact between the two, can be a great alternative to simply dropping crystals into the mix.

Distribution: While many people utilize herbs, flowers, or another tool to distribute the water, you can always use your fingertips in a pinch! Simply dip your herbs/flowers in the water and shake the water off, distributing it around the space.

Incantations: For witches who love to work with the spoken word, there are also a couple of opportunities throughout this process to incorporate an incantation of your choosing. Some whispered words to charge the water with your magical intent, a rhythmic chant repeated throughout the cleansing process, or even a few short and sweet lines to complete the ritual can all add a pop of your personal magic!

While it can be fun to create intricately crafted ritual waters for this practice, all that is truly required is some water and your focused intention. Remember, the magic comes from you!

Record a Card Pull

DECK USED:

_____

CARD(S) PULLED:

_____

_____

_____

YOUR INTERPRETATION:

_____

_____

_____

_____

_____

BOOK INTERPRETATION:

_____

_____

_____

_____

_____

PAUSE & REFLECT

If you could ask a deceased family member one question, what would it be and why would their answer be important to you?

_____

_____

_____

_____

_____

_____

_____

_____

_____

_____

_____

_____

_____

_____

_____

_____

_____

_____

_____

_____

_____

JULY

	M	T	W	T	F	S	S
26	26	27	28	29	30	1	2
27	3	4	5	6	7	8	9
28	10	11	12	13	14	15	16
29	17	18	19	20	21	22	23
30	24	25	26	27	28	29	30
31	31	1	2	3	4	5	6

TO DO LIST

-
-
-
-
-
-
-
-
-

DAILY CARD PULL

Monday

Tuesday

Wednesday

Thursday

Friday

Saturday

Sunday

MONDAY 03

TUESDAY 04 Independence Da

WEDNESDAY 05

THURSDAY 06

2023

FRIDAY	07	

GOALS

SATURDAY	08	

REMEMBER

-
-
-
-
-
-
-

SUNDAY	09	

NOTES

HABITS	M	T	W	T	F	S	S

NEXT WEEK

JULY

	M	T	W	T	F	S	S
26	26	27	28	29	30	1	2
27	3	4	5	6	7	8	9
28	10	11	12	13	14	15	16
29	17	18	19	20	21	22	23
30	24	25	26	27	28	29	30
31	31	1	2	3	4	5	6

TO DO LIST

-
-
-
-
-
-
-
-
-

DAILY CARD PULL

Monday

Tuesday

Wednesday

Thursday

Friday

Saturday

Sunday

MONDAY 10 ☽♈

TUESDAY 11

WEDNESDAY 12

THURSDAY 13

2023

FRIDAY	14	Bastille Day

GOALS

SATURDAY	15	

REMEMBER

-
-
-
-
-
-
-

SUNDAY	16	

NOTES

HABITS	M	T	W	T	F	S	S

NEXT WEEK

JULY

	M	T	W	T	F	S	S
26	26	27	28	29	30	1	2
27	3	4	5	6	7	8	9
28	10	11	12	13	14	15	16
29	17	18	19	20	21	22	23
30	24	25	26	27	28	29	30
31	31	1	2	3	4	5	6

TO DO LIST

-
-
-
-
-
-
-
-
-

DAILY CARD PULL

Monday

Tuesday

Wednesday

Thursday

Friday

Saturday

Sunday

MONDAY 17 ●♋

TUESDAY 18

WEDNESDAY 19

THURSDAY 20

2023

FRIDAY	21		GOALS

SATURDAY	22		REMEMBER

REMEMBER
-
-
-
-
-
-
-

SUNDAY	23	☀️♌	NOTES

HABITS	M	T	W	T	F	S	S	NEXT WEEK

JULY

	M	T	W	T	F	S	S
26	26	27	28	29	30	1	2
27	3	4	5	6	7	8	9
28	10	11	12	13	14	15	16
29	17	18	19	20	21	22	23
30	24	25	26	27	28	29	30
31	31	1	2	3	4	5	6

TO DO LIST

-
-
-
-
-
-
-
-
-

DAILY CARD PULL

Monday

Tuesday

Wednesday

Thursday

Friday

Saturday

Sunday

MONDAY 24

TUESDAY 25

WEDNESDAY 26

THURSDAY 27

2023

FRIDAY	28		GOALS

SATURDAY	29		REMEMBER

REMEMBER
-
-
-
-
-
-
-

SUNDAY	30		NOTES

HABITS	M	T	W	T	F	S	S		NEXT WEEK

GRATITUDE LIST

_____

_____

_____

_____

_____

_____

_____

MONTHLY TO-DO'S

_____

_____

_____

_____

_____

_____

_____

_____

_____

TRY SOMETHING NEW

CRYSTALS
Moonstone is, as the name indicates, strongly connected with the moon, so it's perfect for any magic or rituals requiring lunar energies. The moon is associated with the element of water, which makes it a powerful tool for emotional healing, magic cultivating strength or courage, or enhancing psychic abilities.

CARD SPREAD
Card 1. Home Life – Card 2. Work Life – Card 3. Witch Life

SPELL
Cool Your Body, Clear Your Mind: Find a river, stream, or just use your shower, so long as it's flowing, and cool. Imagine, as the water washes over you, all the stressors in life washing away. They're being taken by the water to be recycled, put to good use for Mother Earth.

ENTITY
Go outside and mingle with the nature spirits around your home. Let your intuition guide your exploration, using your psychic abilities to connect and communicate with spirits of trees, flowers, rocks, the land itself.

SELF-CARE
Go on a date...with yourself. Take time to get ready, take great care in choosing your outfit, groom meticulously. Go out for a fancy dinner or cook yourself a decadent meal. Watch your favorite movie, or sit and watch the sunset, holding your own hand. Be sure to kiss yourself goodnight...or go further, no one will judge you.

TEA chai
Chai is an easy and delicious blend of black tea, dried orange peel, cinnamon and clove. Cinnamon draws success and money, while clove provides powerful protective energies.

HERBS
Poultices, tinctures, and infusions are common techniques for herbal magic. A poultice is when a fresh herb is crushed into a pulp and applied to a warm cloth, moistened with either fresh or salt water, that is applied to an injury. A tincture is a concentrated herbal extract, made by soaking fresh leaves, berries, and/or roots of one or more plants in alcohol or vinegar, and either taken orally, or used topically. Infusions are made by soaking or steeping either dried or fresh herbs in water, pulling the flavor and medicinal properties from the herbs.

Record a Card Pull

DECK USED:

_____

CARD(S) PULLED:

_____

_____

_____

YOUR INTERPRETATION:

_____

_____

_____

_____

_____

_____

BOOK INTERPRETATION:

_____

_____

_____

_____

_____

"Those that can heal can harm; those that can cure can kill."

- Celia Rees

August

Calendar Key
- 🌕 Full Moon
- 🌑 New Moon
- 🌓 First Quarter
- 🌗 Last Quarter
- Eclipse
- Sun

Goals

Notes

Monday	Tuesday	Wednesday
	1 — 213/152 — Lammas	2 — 214/151
7 — 219/146	8 — 220/145	9 — 221/144
14 — 226/139	15 — 227/138	16 — 228/137
21 — 233/132	22 — 234/131	23 — 235/130
28 — 240/125	29 — 241/124	30 — 242/123

AUGUST

M	T	W	T	F	S	S
	1	2	3	4	5	6
7	8	9	10	11	12	13
14	15	16	17	18	19	20
21	22	23	24	25	26	27
28	29	30	31			

Thursday	Friday	Saturday	Sunday
3 215/150	4 216/149	5 217/148	6 218/147
0 222/143	11 223/142	12 224/141	13 225/140
7 229/136	18 230/135	19 231/134	20 232/133
4 236/129	25 237/128	26 238/127	27 239/126
1 243/122			

LUNAR PHASES

AUGUST 1ST: FULL MOON IN AQUARIUS

The moon in Aquarius gives us the need for emotional freedoms which can cause complications in our relationships. Can also be a time when you are able to better understand your emotions, freeing you from negative feelings such as jealousy, fear, and anger.

AUGUST 8TH: LAST QUARTER IN TAURUS

Your sense of safety arises from the need for stability which is difficult to find at the moment. The key to stability is acceptance – accepting that change is a part of life, and acceptance of who you are as a person. When you accept yourself you will find that peace and tranquility are much easier to come by in your daily life.

AUGUST 16TH: NEW MOON IN LEO

Your sense of safety arises from the need for stability which is difficult to find at the moment. The key to stability is acceptance – accepting that change is a part of life, and acceptance of who you are as a person. When you accept yourself you will find that peace and tranquility are much easier to come by in your daily life.

AUGUST 24TH: FIRST QUARTER IN SAGITTARIUS

The moon in Sagittarius is the most optimistic of energies, giving you a craving for new experiences and adventure. Motivations under the Sagittarius moon are driven by the need for the truth, or finding something, be it a philosophy, a goal or new hobby. You may be inclined to overdo things, so make sure you don't forget to count your blessings and appreciate what you have right now.

AUGUST 31ST: FULL MOON IN PISCES
(BLUE MOON)

The moon in Pisces is a great time for a creative or spiritual quest, as the energy heightens your emotional sensitivity and perception of your surroundings. Be mindful of feelings of insecurity. Should you begin to feel insecure just be patient and open to letting events unfold as they come.

RITUAL PLANNER

GOAL/INTENTION:

_____

_____

_____

ITEMS NEEDED:

_____

_____

_____

_____

_____

STEPS:

_____

_____

_____

_____

AUGUST HERBS

Growing the herbs listed above in a window garden would serve any kitchen witch well as they offer a number of magical properties. Whether you need to work magic for health or wealth, for protection or strength, to aid with spirit work or get in touch with the Divine- even if you want to work a glamour or weight loss spell, you'll be covered.

You'll need air-tight containers to store the herbs once you harvest and dry them. Mason jars are excellent for this purpose. I recommend purchasing a sheet of jar labels as well, recording the kind of herb and the date they were dried. Herbs dried and stored in air-tight containers will retain their flavor for up to a year.

You may wish to get a mortar and pestle reserved solely for magical purposes, as it can become charged with your magic, amplifying the power of the herbs ground within it (that's how it seems to work for me anyways).

HERB	SIZE/ SPREAD	START SEEDS INSIDE/OUTSIDE	HARDINESS ZONE	NATIVE REGION	GROWTH TYPE**	SUN/ SOIL*
Thyme	2-12"/7-12"	6-10/2-3	5-9	Paleartic regions of Europe and Asia	P	FS/WI
Oregano	12-24"/18"	6-10	5-12	Mediterranean region of West Asia	P	FS/WI
Parsley	18-24"/6-8"	10-12/3-4 After	4-9	Mediterranean regions of South Eruope and West Asia	B	PS/R
Chives	12-18"	8-10/3-4	3-12	Temperate areas of Europe, Asia and North America	P	FS/RM

*Weeks before or afer last spring frost

** A=Annual P=Perennial

** FS= full sun; PS= partial sun; WD= well-drained, M= moist, RM, rich moint, L= loamy, LS=loamy/sandy

Magic Properties:
Thyme: Good Health, Loyalty, Affection, Strength, Courage, Improve Finances
Oregano: Joy, Strength, Vitality and Added Energy
Parsley: Death, Rebirth, Connecting with Higher Self
Chives: Protection, Weight Loss

SWIMMING MEDITATIONS

By Jessica Marie Baumgartner

Summer is a time for sunshine, growth, and heat. Not everyone handles hot sticky weather the same way, but in order to enjoy the great outdoors and cool down, water is one of the most magical elements during this season.

All a person needs to enjoy the power and guidance of water is their body and their will. There are many state and national parks with open swimming areas. If this does not suit you, local pools work well, and some meditations can even be modified for a bathtub or shower.

The point isn't to stress about location; it is mainly to connect to the water's power and allow that constant force to aid you in finding peace. This is such an important element of my life that I wrote an entire chapter of it in my book, The Magic of Nature. There are different levels of immersion, meant to accommodate people of various backgrounds, but they are all things I began doing without realizing it at first.

For anyone who is not a great swimmer, or even a bit weary of water, this simple meditation can be done in a tub or shallow body of water like a stream or creek:

1. Clear your mind. Breathe deep and walk into the water. Ankle deep is enough, but up to the waist is good if comfortable. Stand or sit as comfortably as possible.
2. Focus your energies on the here and now. Meditate on enjoying the space. Let the atmosphere encompass you.
3. Imagine the source of your energy being refreshed and replenished by the water's movement.
4. Gaze up into the sky. Breathe in and clear your mind. Breathe out and look to the water. Focus on the images reflected. Take plenty of time.
5. Think of the current, ripples, or bubbles as friends welcoming you.
6. Let the gentle voice of nature speak to you. Listen for as long as possible.

PAUSE & REFLECT

List the places that you long to go and the reasons why.

_____

_____

_____

_____

_____

_____

_____

_____

_____

_____

_____

_____

_____

_____

_____

_____

_____

_____

_____

_____

_____

AUGUST FESTIVALS

August 1st is marked as the Celtic holiday Lughnasadh. This holiday was originally celebrated in Ireland, Scotland, and the Isle of Man to mark the beginning of the harvest season. Festivities consisted of competitions and feasts, celebrating love and appreciation for the land, for kin, and for spirits. According to Irish mythology, the very first Lughnasadh was organized by the god Lugh himself in honor of his foster mother, Tailtiu. Tailtiu cleared the way for the introduction of agriculture in Ireland, so there would be no harvest if it weren't for her.
[Source: https://druidry.org/druid-way/teaching-and-practice/druid-festivals/lughnasadh]

USE THE SPACE BELOW TO RECORD YOUR AUGUST CELEBRATIONS

AUGUST

	M	T	W	T	F	S	S
31	31	1	2	3	4	5	6
32	7	8	9	10	11	12	13
33	14	15	16	17	18	19	20
34	21	22	23	24	25	26	27
35	28	29	30	31	1	2	3

TO DO LIST

-
-
-
-
-
-
-
-
-

DAILY CARD PULL

Monday

Tuesday

Wednesday

Thursday

Friday

Saturday

Sunday

MONDAY 31

TUESDAY 01 Lammas

WEDNESDAY 02

THURSDAY 03

2023

FRIDAY 04

GOALS

SATURDAY 05

REMEMBER

-
-
-
-
-
-
-

SUNDAY 06

NOTES

HABITS

	M	T	W	T	F	S	S

NEXT WEEK

AUGUST

	M	T	W	T	F	S	S
31	31	1	2	3	4	5	6
32	7	8	9	10	11	12	13
33	14	15	16	17	18	19	20
34	21	22	23	24	25	26	27
35	28	29	30	31	1	2	3

TO DO LIST

-
-
-
-
-
-
-
-
-

DAILY CARD PULL

- Monday
- Tuesday
- Wednesday
- Thursday
- Friday
- Saturday
- Sunday

MONDAY 07

TUESDAY 08

WEDNESDAY 09

THURSDAY 10

2023

FRIDAY	11		GOALS

SATURDAY	12		REMEMBER

REMEMBER
-
-
-
-
-
-
-

SUNDAY	13		NOTES

HABITS	M	T	W	T	F	S	S	NEXT WEEK

AUGUST

	M	T	W	T	F	S	S
31	31	1	2	3	4	5	6
32	7	8	9	10	11	12	13
33	14	15	16	17	18	19	20
34	21	22	23	24	25	26	27
35	28	29	30	31	1	2	3

TO DO LIST

-
-
-
-
-
-
-
-
-

DAILY CARD PULL

Monday

Tuesday

Wednesday

Thursday

Friday

Saturday

Sunday

MONDAY	14	

TUESDAY	15	

WEDNESDAY	16 ●♌	

THURSDAY	17	

2023

FRIDAY	18		GOALS

SATURDAY	19		REMEMBER

-
-
-
-
-
-
-

SUNDAY	20		NOTES

HABITS	M	T	W	T	F	S	S	NEXT WEEK

AUGUST

	M	T	W	T	F	S	S
31	31	1	2	3	4	5	6
32	7	8	9	10	11	12	13
33	14	15	16	17	18	19	20
34	21	22	23	24	25	26	27
35	28	29	30	31	1	2	3

TO DO LIST

-
-
-
-
-
-
-
-
-

DAILY CARD PULL

Monday

Tuesday

Wednesday

Thursday

Friday

Saturday

Sunday

MONDAY 21 ☀︎ ♍

TUESDAY 22

WEDNESDAY 23

THURSDAY 24 ☽ ♐

2023

FRIDAY	25		GOALS

SATURDAY	26		REMEMBER

-
-
-
-
-
-
-

SUNDAY	27		NOTES

HABITS	M	T	W	T	F	S	S	NEXT WEEK

AUGUST

	M	T	W	T	F	S	S
31	31	1	2	3	4	5	6
32	7	8	9	10	11	12	13
33	14	15	16	17	18	19	20
34	21	22	23	24	25	26	27
35	28	29	30	31	1	2	3

TO DO LIST

-
-
-
-
-
-
-
-
-

DAILY CARD PULL

Monday

Tuesday

Wednesday

Thursday

Friday

Saturday

Sunday

MONDAY   28

TUESDAY   29

WEDNESDAY   30

THURSDAY   31   )(

2023

FRIDAY | 01

GOALS

SATURDAY | 02

REMEMBER

-
-
-
-
-
-
-

SUNDAY | 03

NOTES

HABITS

	M	T	W	T	F	S	S

NEXT WEEK

GRATITUDE LIST

_____

_____

_____

_____

_____

_____

_____

MONTHLY TO-DO'S

_____

_____

_____

_____

_____

_____

_____

_____

_____

_____

TRY SOMETHING NEW

CRYSTALS
Making crystal wards is a simple and effective technique for protective magic. Simply choose four or more crystals with protective properties. Cleanse them, charge them, and place them at even intervals around the boundary of the room, home, or space that needs protecting.

CARD SPREAD
Card 1. Think – Card 2. Feel – Card 3. Do

SPELL
Tarot charms are a simple and effective spell-casting technique. You simply choose a tarot card with the archetype or energy that would manifest your will, charge the card as you would any crystal or tool, and keep the card with you until your will has been manifested or your need has been met. For example, the Chariot will sharpen your focus, the Lovers will help you resolve conflict with another person.

ENTITY
Light aspecting, or invoking, is when you invite an aspect of a deity or entity into your body, remaining conscious and in control of your actions, bolstered by the power you've got nestled inside. Study various techniques and explore- with caution. Great for sexual prowess, confidence, courage, and standing firm in your position.

SELF-CARE
Go through your closet and/or dresser and pull out any clothes you don't wear anymore. Send half to charity and take the other half to a consignment shop. Use the money you make from consigning your clothes to get yourself something new, something that makes you feel sexy, powerful, and attractive.

TEA
When you want to make tea for a specific purpose, make an herbal tea based on the properties of the herbs, or a classic tea and rely on the properties of additives. If you want to attract money, for example, a peppermint tea with honey will not only attract money but will help it stick. A ginger tea with lemon is great for instilling strength, cultivating courage, and tapping into your personal power. A chocolate tea with rose hips and strawberries will make the ultimate love potion.

HERBS
Comfrey has powerful healing properties and is excellent for topical use to treat swelling, burns, and lacerations. The energies of this herb offer protection and encourage a sense of adventure, so it's the perfect herb for workings involving travel, journeys, or exploration.

Record a Card Pull

DECK USED:

_____

CARD(S) PULLED:

_____

_____

_____

YOUR INTERPRETATION:

_____

_____

_____

_____

_____

_____

BOOK INTERPRETATION:

_____

_____

_____

_____

_____

_____

"We can see the Divine in each speck of dust, but that doesn't stop us from wiping it away with a wet sponge. The Divine doesn't disappear; it's transformed into the clean surface."

- Paulo Coelho

September

Calendar Key
- 🌑 Full Moon
- ⚫ New Moon
- 🌓 First Quarter
- 🌗 Last Quarter
- 🌘 Eclipse
- ☀ Sun

AUGUST

M	T	W	T	F	S	S
	1	2	3	4	5	6
7	8	9	10	11	12	13
14	15	16	17	18	19	20
21	22	23	24	25	26	27
28	29	30	31			

OCTOBER

M	T	W	T	F	S	S
30	31					1
2	3	4	5	6	7	8
9	10	11	12	13	14	15
16	17	18	19	20	21	22
23	24	25	26	27	28	29

Goals

Notes

	Monday	Tuesday	Wednesday
	4 247/118	5 248/117	6 249/116 🌓♊
	11 254/111	12 255/110	13 256/109
	18 261/104	19 262/103	20 263/102
	25 268/97	26 269/96	27 270/95

SEPTEMBER

M	T	W	T	F	S	S
				1	2	3
4	5	6	7	8	9	10
11	12	13	14	15	16	17
18	19	20	21	22	23	24
25	26	27	28	29	30	

Thursday	Friday	Saturday	Sunday
	1 244/121	**2** 245/120	**3** 246/119
7 250/115	**8** 251/114	**9** 252/113	**10** 253/112
14 257/108	**15** 258/107	**16** 259/106	**17** 260/105
21 264/101	**22** 265/100	**23** 266/99 Fall Equinox	**24** 267/98
28 271/94	**29** 272/93	**30** 273/92	

LUNAR PHASES

SEPTEMBER 6TH: LAST QUARTER IN GEMINI

Under the Gemini moon you may find that communicating your feelings and emotions becomes easier. Your actions are motivated by the desire for variety and the urge to satisfy curiosity. Just be careful you don't become reckless and fickle – the key is harmony of the mind and heart.

SEPTEMBER 15TH: NEW MOON IN VIRGO

The Virgo moon is one of order and practicality. You feel you have to reorganize and bring order to anything you feel is in chaos. This can lead to being intolerant of others, so try focusing more on solving problems, creating order within your life, and helping others without judgement.

SEPTEMBER 22ND: FIRST QUARTER IN SAGITTARIUS

The moon in Sagittarius is the most optimistic of energies, giving you a craving for new experiences and adventure. Motivations under the Sagittarius moon are driven by the need for the truth, or finding something, be it a philosophy, a goal or new hobby. You may be inclined to overdo things, so make sure you don't forget to count your blessings and appreciate what you have right now.

SEPTEMBER 29TH: FULL MOON IN ARIES

The moon in Aries is emotionally direct and impulsive, with strong, influential feelings. Time for a fresh start, learning new behaviors, establishing new habits. Just don't rush to make decisions, as Aries is apt to do, feeling as though quicker is better. It's not. Take your time to consider what you need, what you want, and choose carefully. The choices made in Aries set the tone for the extended future.

RITUAL PLANNER

GOAL/INTENTION:

_____

_____

_____

ITEMS NEEDED:

_____

_____

_____

_____

_____

STEPS:

_____

_____

_____

_____

SEPTEMBER HERB PLANTING GUIDE: THE COLORFUL AND CREATIVE COTTAGE GARDEN

The cottage garden design is the quintessential witch garden, in my opinion. It's creative, it's colorful, it's free and wild, and has the perfect balance of prettiness and practicality. It's the perfect design for witches because it's magical, it's useful, it's helpful, and it's beneficial to the surrounding land and local critters.

The Cottage garden originated as a means to maximize usefulness, consisting mainly of edible and medicinal plants. People without money or means to get food or medicine grew as much as they could fit within their tiny bit of land. Today, people plant cottage gardens more for pleasure and aesthetics than they do for practicality.
A cottage garden design consists of a diverse variety of plants that appeals to all senses, with pleasing aromas, bright and cheery colors, a range of textures and an assortment of shapes and sizes. The garden has an optimistic, laid back, and welcoming spirit. The plants may appear as though their seeds were mixed up and thrown into the soil at random, but placement is important. It's an organized chaos, but one that gardeners with any level of experience can achieve with a bit of consideration, contemplation, and planning.

Suggestions for Cottage Garden Creation

Based on personal experience and research, I've learned that you can create and maintain a happy and healthy cottage garden by keeping a few key suggestions in mind. First and foremost: start small! You can always add more to the garden later, but you don't want to turn half your yard into a cottage garden just to have half of it die before June. Planting in front of a picket fence or lattice slat would give the garden structure, make a picturesque backdrop, and provide the opportunity to include a climbing plant (i.e. climbing roses, wisteria, morning glories). Planting flowering shrubs, small fruit trees, or ornamental grasses would also provide structure. Adding a structural component adds a bit of order to the chaos. For enticing aromas plant a variety of herbs.

When choosing flowers, TheGardeningCook.com says that an assortment of tall flowering perennials, hardy biennials, and self-seeding annuals will "give your garden just the right look". Examples of tall flowering perennials include Bellflower, Phlox, and Delphinium; hardy biennials include Foxglove, Forget Me Nots, and Sweet William; and self-seeding annuals include Calendula, Bachelor Button, and Poppies. Repeating colors and patterns would maintain the chaotic look with

Source List/Suggested Reading:
https://www.bhg.com/gardening/yard/garden-care/cottage-garden-care/ https://www.gardendesign.com/cottage/ideas.html
https://www.thespruce.com/creating-a-cottage-garden-1402541
https://thegardeningcook.com/30-cottage-garden-plants-for-your-garden/

Record a Card Pull

DECK USED:

_____

CARD(S) PULLED:

_____

_____

_____

YOUR INTERPRETATION:

_____

_____

_____

_____

_____

_____

BOOK INTERPRETATION:

_____

_____

_____

_____

_____

_____

Found-Object Divination

Incorporating charm casting into your divination practice involves a series of steps, the first two preparatory in nature and the final being the practice itself. Here is a brief overview of the process:

1.   Curation of lots collection: Finding the lots, establishing definitions for each item, and creating a written record of each item and the meanings and associations you've attributed to them—a sort of dictionary, if you will.

2.   Practice preparation: Procurement of casting cloth, optional collection/creation of casting circle cloth, and sheets (fabric or cloth) to serve as guides for various spreads.

3.   Initiate found-object divination practice: Optional precursory ritual to charge, bless, cleanse, or otherwise energetically and magically charge the lots.

Step 1: Curating Your Collection of Lots

Lots are magical tools that read into the energies and powers surrounding the question and that respond in a way reflecting how those energies and powers interact with your life. Gathering items for your collection is more than just picking random do-dads from around your house—they must catch your eye and must feel significant in some way (even if you aren't sure what it is yet).

One way to ensure that you've found objects meant for your collection is to practice mindfulness. Mindfulness enables you to absorb what your physical senses experience and then accurately comprehend your intuitive response. You're more likely to notice things meant for you—and more able to differentiate between significant items and items you happened to find—if you're being mindful. Intention setting is another helpful approach. You can give yourself a purpose, either for the day or for an activity. To set an intention for the day, for example, right when you wake up you can tell yourself that you will find an object for your collection—or you can tell yourself that your eyes are going to be sharp, easily spotting any objects meant for you.

In researching this practice, I've come across a few articles that offer different instructions for finding the lots. One suggested limiting the number of lots to nine or thirteen. There was an article that advised creating a list of qualities to meet, i.e., one lot each for wealth, health, change, obstacles, relationships, etc. Another source stated to simply be mindful of the meanings, making sure that each aspect of life, both positive and negative, is covered. Personally, I think whatever meanings you intuit from the lots you find are going to be relevant to you and your life, so you shouldn't force associations to meet someone else's standards.

The final aspect to address is storage. Deciding what you'll put the lots in and where to keep it can be done at any time. You can keep the lots in any container, such as a pouch, box, or bag. Whatever you decide, I recommend cleansing it before you put the lots inside. This prevents energy contamination. You should cleanse the area where you'll keep the box or bag of lots as well. Energy isn't tangible but can easily attach itself to the lots, regardless of whether they're in a cloth bag or a steel box. You want your divination tools to be effective. Stagnant, distracting energies can interfere with the tool's objective.

Step 2: Practice Setup & Preparation

With the collection complete and associations or meanings attributed, set the box or bag of lots aside. While the lots spend some quality time together in their storage container, you will continue setting up your practice, moving on to acquire the cloth/plate/etc. onto which you'll cast the lots. You may wish to get a nice altar cloth made of felt, canvas, or some other soft, thick material to lay down over the table; the fabric will absorb the shock and protect any fragile items from shattering on the table. While the protective cloth is sufficient for the practice, you may choose to cast the lots onto difference spreads.

Spreads for lot casting work much like that of spreads for tarot or rune stones. On a square of thin cotton or cotton/ poly blend fabric, you'll first lay down a large circle. Any lots landing outside the circle may either be disregarded or interpreted as external factors influencing the situation. You could divide the circle into quadrants, drawing intersecting lines to create four equal quarters. You could write what each quadrant represents on the cloth itself, or you can create a variety of spreads and keep notes in your journal, grimoire, or book of shadows to remind yourself of what each quadrant position signifies for each spread. Another option is to use actual tarot spreads, drawing lots for each location (as opposed to casting all of them onto the work surface). This could be as complex as drawing and placing lots in the form of the Celtic cross spread or as simple as drawing three circles or squares in a row, writing the significance of each one within the shape itself.

You can have as many or as few casting cloths or spread guides as you want. I would recommend storing them in their own bag or box, which you'll keep with the lots container. As you did with the lots container, cleanse the bag or box before storing the cloths and spread designs inside. You could cleanse and charge the cloths if you want as well.

Exquisite Experience

This method of divination can take some getting used to. There's no guidebook, no suggested meanings. There's no template to follow advising the kinds of objects to collect, and no rules telling you how many. You must rely solely on your intuition—take the opportunity to refine your psychic senses and let your trust in yourself grow.

Unlike purchasing a deck of tarot cards or rune stones, building a collection of found objects entails an investment of time and energies, providing you with a ready-made set of divinatory tools with predetermined meanings. Sure, the latter would be easier. But the precise and mindful approach toward building your collection will result in a one-of-a-kind set of tools infused with your magic and tailored to your energies and spirit. To experience a reading with a set of tools such as that will be well worth the investment.

PAUSE & REFLECT

Think about and list things that made your childhood magical.

_____

_____

_____

_____

_____

_____

_____

_____

_____

_____

_____

_____

_____

_____

_____

_____

_____

_____

_____

_____

_____

SEPTEMBER FESTIVALS

The 15th day of the 8th month of the Chinese lunisolar calendar, (which falls in either September or November of the Gregorian calendar), the Moon festival is celebrated by people of East and Southeast Asia. The Moon festival, or the Mid-Autumn Festival, originated 3000 years ago when the Chinese worshipped the moon, revering it as a symbol of peace and prosperity, and held the festival to gain the moons' blessing for a bountiful harvest. Today, the Moon Festival is celebrated by carrying or displaying lanterns of all shapes and sizes as symbolic beacons, guiding people towards prosperity and good fortune. The traditional food of the Moon festival is the moon cake, which is a pastry filled with either sweet-bean or lotus-seed paste.

The Moon festival is known as Chuseok, "Autumn Eve", in Korea (both North and South), Tsukimi, "Moon Viewing", in Japan, and Tét Trung Thu, "Mid-Autumn Festival", in Vietnam.

[Source: https://en.wikipedia.org/wiki/Mid-AutumnFestival]

USE THE SPACE BELOW TO RECORD YOUR SEPTEMBER CELEBRATIONS

SEPTEMBER

	M	T	W	T	F	S	S
35	28	29	30	31	1	2	3
36	4	5	6	7	8	9	10
37	11	12	13	14	15	16	17
38	18	19	20	21	22	23	24
39	25	26	27	28	29	30	1

TO DO LIST

-
-
-
-
-
-
-
-
-

DAILY CARD PULL

Monday

Tuesday

Wednesday

Thursday

Friday

Saturday

Sunday

MONDAY	04	Labor Day

TUESDAY	05	

WEDNESDAY	06	

THURSDAY	07	

2023

FRIDAY	08		GOALS

SATURDAY	09		REMEMBER

REMEMBER
-
-
-
-
-
-
-

SUNDAY	10		NOTES

HABITS	M	T	W	T	F	S	S	NEXT WEEK

SEPTEMBER

	M	T	W	T	F	S	S
35	28	29	30	31	1	2	3
36	4	5	6	7	8	9	10
37	11	12	13	14	15	16	17
38	18	19	20	21	22	23	24
39	25	26	27	28	29	30	1

TO DO LIST

-
-
-
-
-
-
-
-
-

DAILY CARD PULL

Monday

Tuesday

Wednesday

Thursday

Friday

Saturday

Sunday

MONDAY · 11

TUESDAY · 12

WEDNESDAY · 13

THURSDAY · 14

2023

FRIDAY	15	●♍	Rosh Hashangh, Begins at Sunset

GOALS

SATURDAY	16

REMEMBER

-
-
-
-
-
-
-

SUNDAY	17

NOTES

HABITS	M	T	W	T	F	S	S

NEXT WEEK

SEPTEMBER

	M	T	W	T	F	S	S
35	28	29	30	31	1	2	3
36	4	5	6	7	8	9	10
37	11	12	13	14	15	16	17
38	18	19	20	21	22	23	24
39	25	26	27	28	29	30	1

TO DO LIST

-
-
-
-
-
-
-
-
-

DAILY CARD PULL

Monday

Tuesday

Wednesday

Thursday

Friday

Saturday

Sunday

MONDAY 18

TUESDAY 19

WEDNESDAY 20

THURSDAY 21

2023

FRIDAY	22	🌓♐	

SATURDAY	23	☀♎	Autumn Equinox

REMEMBER

-
-
-
-
-
-
-

SUNDAY	24		Yom Kippur, Begins at Sunset

NOTES

HABITS

	M	T	W	T	F	S	S

NEXT WEEK

SEPTEMBER

	M	T	W	T	F	S	S
35	28	29	30	31	1	2	3
36	4	5	6	7	8	9	10
37	11	12	13	14	15	16	17
38	18	19	20	21	22	23	24
39	25	26	27	28	29	30	1

TO DO LIST

-
-
-
-
-
-
-
-
-

DAILY CARD PULL

Monday

Tuesday

Wednesday

Thursday

Friday

Saturday

Sunday

MONDAY 25

TUESDAY 26

WEDNESDAY 27

THURSDAY 28

2023

FRIDAY	29 ☾♈

GOALS

SATURDAY	30

REMEMBER

-
-
-
-
-
-
-

SUNDAY	01

NOTES

HABITS

	M	T	W	T	F	S	S

NEXT WEEK

GRATITUDE LIST

_____

_____

_____

_____

_____

_____

_____

MONTHLY TO-DO'S

_____

_____

_____

_____

_____

_____

_____

_____

_____

TRY SOMETHING NEW

CRYSTALS
Pearl is the perfect stone to overcome obstacles, aid with perseverance, and learning to be more adaptable. This potent energy comes from the pearls' creation, starting as a grain of sand, or some other irritant, that made its' way into an oyster shell, which the oyster then coats with calcium and aragonite in order to ease the irritation. The oyster patiently coats and forms and smooths until its' pain has eased.

CARD SPREAD
Card 1. Save it – Card 2. Sell it - Card 3. Salvage it

SPELL:
When it comes to working magic, the items needed are typically required because of the energies they're associated with. This means that your spell can be just as effective even if you don't have the required items, so long as you include substitutes that draw the same associations. If you can't like a green candle, you can use a battery powered candle – if you're really in a bind, a drawing or picture of a green candle will suffice.

ENTITY
There are Shamanic practices in which magic is carried out by working with spirits relevant to your intention – i.e., working with spirits of the sky to ensure a safe flight. Research various methods as inspiration for techniques you can incorporate into your practices, (just be sure to be mindful of originating cultures, respecting their ways and attributing credit where credit is due.)

SELF-CARE
Enact a daily "you" time. From_o'clock to_o'clock, no noise, no children, no pets, nothing, will bother you. You work hard and you deserve a break, EVERY DAY.

TEA
Getting into the habit of performing rituals for devotion, inspiration, or any other intention, can be tricky. Getting into a routine with tea would resolve that issue, and would be an easy habit to form. It's best to have your tea routine in the morning, since any black tea will be loaded with caffeine, but it's down to personal preference as to when you do it. Choose your teas based on the properties of the ingredients, and practice mindfulness, visualization, and grounding and centering while you sit peacefully, enjoying your tea.

HERBS
Apples, in ancient times, were a symbol of immortality and harvest, believed to have a strong connection to the Spirit world and its' inhabitants. This believe has been carried on through the generations, as apples, as well as apple blossoms, are often used in divination, love magic, and spirit work.

Record a Card Pull

DECK USED:

_____

CARD(S) PULLED:

_____

_____

_____

YOUR INTERPRETATION:

_____

_____

_____

_____

_____

_____

BOOK INTERPRETATION:

_____

_____

_____

_____

_____

_____

"We are the gods of our own universes, aren't we?
Destructive ones."

- Olivie Blake

October

Calendar Key
- Full Moon
- New Moon
- First Quarter
- Last Quarter
- Eclipse
- Sun

SEPTEMBER

M	T	W	T	F	S	S
				1	2	3
4	5	6	7	8	9	10
11	12	13	14	15	16	17
18	19	20	21	22	23	24
25	26	27	28	29	30	

NOVEMBER

M	T	W	T	F	S	S
	1	2	3	4	5	
6	7	8	9	10	11	12
13	14	15	16	17	18	19
20	21	22	23	24	25	26
27	28	29	30			

Goals

Notes

Monday	Tuesday	Wednesday
2 275/90	**3** 276/89	**4** 277/88
9 282/83 Indigenous Peoples' Day	**10** 283/82	**11** 284/81
16 289/76	**17** 290/75	**18** 291/74
23 296/69	**24** 297/68	**25** 298/67
30	**31** Samhain	

OCTOBER

M	T	W	T	F	S	S
30	31					1
2	3	4	5	6	7	8
9	10	11	12	13	14	15
16	17	18	19	20	21	22
23	24	25	26	27	28	29

Thursday	Friday	Saturday	Sunday
			1 274/91
5 278/87	**6** 279/86	**7** 280/85	**8** 281/84
2 285/80	**13** 286/79	**14** 287/78	**15** 288/77
9 292/73	**20** 293/72	**21** 294/71	**22** 295/70
6 299/66	**27** 300/65	**28** 301/64	**29** 302/63

LUNAR PHASES

OCTOBER 6TH: LAST QUARTER IN CANCER

The Moon in Cancer instills in you emotional security and a sense of belonging, a sense of nurturing you feel instinctively. You find that you're longing for an intimate connection that's meaningful and long-lasting, enough so you can establish a sense of belonging-put down roots, a place to bunker down as the Universe throws its' trials and tribulations at you. Using the Full Moon energies to work a self-love spell may help to satisfy this desire.

OCTOBER 14TH: NEW MOON IN LIBRA

The moon in Libra drives us for a sense of order, but unlike that of the moon in Virgo, we are satisfied by pleasant interactions and aesthetics in the environment. The need for order and harmony are strong, and rather than deal with confrontation you try to keep everything 'nice'. Don't let the Libra moon make you forget who you are, and certainly resist the urge to bottle up your feelings.

OCTOBER 22ND: FIRST QUARTER IN AQUARIUS

The moon in Aquarius gives us the need for emotional freedoms which can cause complications in our relationships. Can also be a time when you are able to better understand your emotions, freeing you from negative feelings such as jealousy, fear, and anger.

OCTOBER 28TH: FULL MOON IN TAURUS

Your sense of safety arises from the need for stability which is difficult to find at the moment. The key to stability is acceptance – accepting that change is a part of life, and acceptance of who you are as a person. When you accept yourself you will find that peace and tranquility are much easier to come by in your daily life.

RITUAL PLANNER

GOAL/INTENTION:

_____

_____

_____

ITEMS NEEDED:

_____

_____

_____

_____

_____

STEPS:

_____

_____

_____

_____

THE SILENT SUPPER: A FEAST FOR ANCESTORS

by Kiki Dombrowski

Suppose you are looking for a profound way to honor your ancestors while dining. In that case, the Silent Supper may be a supernatural and magical activity to try out. The Silent Supper, sometimes known as the Silent Supper, is a special meal that is prepared, arranged, and served with an extra special guest: the spirit of someone close to you who has passed over. The premise of the Silent Supper is simple:

-Create a delectable feast.

-Set an extra place for the spirit you are commemorating.

-Have the meal in silence.

The word "Silent" is used to refer to the fact that the meal takes place in complete silence. While a Silent Supper can technically be hosted at any time, it is commonly associated with the season of Samhain, when we honor ancestors and the world of the dead. Here are a few additional ideas that can help you plan for hosting a Silent Supper.

The History of the Silent Supper

While modern Pagans and witches have revered the Silent Supper as a tradition to feast with the dearly departed, the Silent Supper has folkloric roots in love divination. There is little evidence to even indicate that the Silent Supper had ancient origins, deeply seeded in a distant Pagan World. That being said, what we do see historically is still fascinating and worth considering.

The accounts of the divinatory Silent Supper have appeared in the British Isles and America. However, many Silent Supper games have been connected to Appalachian and Ozark regions, especially in rural locations during Victorian times. Two unmarried young ladies would sweep, clean, cook, sit at the table and wait in silence. At the end of the meal, it was believed that the vision of a person would clearly appear – this person would be one of the ladies' future mates. Other accounts say that the future husband would walk through the door at midnight. This Silent Supper has come with a range of strange procedures for participants to see results, including doing activities backward (such as serving dessert first), preparing food behind your back, and even throwing freshly clipped nails into a fire. Some even warned that seeing a coffin at the end of the Silent Supper was an unfortunate omen of death. While modern Pagans have created the Silent Supper into a more reverent ritual than a divination game, both versions still possess a supernatural energy. However, the contemporary rendition focuses on honoring the Dead, celebrating their memories, and possibly having a spiritual encounter with them.

Honoring the Dead

Before you begin to prepare for your Silent Supper, consider someone who has passed away that you would like to honor. Know that they are coming to have dinner with you in spirit, so consider what you would like to do in their presence and why you wish to have them present. And, a special note: you are certainly welcome to invite dearly departed pets. Anyone who has lost a loved pet knows that they are also special and vital family members.

Preparing Your Space and Table Settings

Have a tidy and clean space to host the meal – if you chose to, consider purifying the space with incense or wiping the table with rose water. Use this special feast as an opportunity to express your decorative spirit. If you are hosting this during the Samhain season, incorporate symbols that you associate with your Samhain practices, for example, pumpkins and black or orange candles. This is also your opportunity to include decorations you associate with the person you honor for the feast. This could mean decorating with photos of the person or even featuring personal effects, like jewelry or their heirloom dining ware. Assign seating ahead of time, ensuring that one seat is left for the spirit you honor at the meal.

The Food and Offerings

It has always been said that you should prepare the favorite foods of the person you are honoring at the Silent Supper. Think about what you would cook for them if they were alive. If you are honoring someone who was a cook while alive, consider using his/her/their personal recipes. You may also want to consider including additional offerings to welcome the people you are honoring. This may include a favorite beverage prepared to their liking, cigarettes or tobacco, flowers, or special personal items that you've crafted. If you are preparing a space for dear pets who have passed over, consider where they feel most welcome. You may have an old feeding dish or favorite blanket that you can set up in a cozy spot for your pet to also feel welcome to visit. Consider welcoming them with a favorite toy or treat or a particular food item they enjoyed on special occasions while alive.

The Silent Supper

The Silent Supper should be a calmer event. Not one could be interrupted with high energy, distractions, or loud noises. The Silent Supper itself has been described in a variety of ways – perhaps you can determine which method feels suitable for your celebration. The traditional method used for a Silent Supper is to have the meal in complete silence. This is said to be a way to show reverence for those who have passed away. This serves as a time to quietly reflect on the person who passed and as an opportunity to listen for any sounds that would indicate the spirit being present.
In contrast, some believe that the Silent Supper has moments of conversation and sound. There may be times where favorite music is played, or favorite memories and funny stories are shared. Perhaps these conversations can be had as a way to open the meal or to close the feast. While there are silent moments, see if you experience anything that would indicate that a spirit is present. Perhaps there is a temperature change,

or you smell their favorite perfume. Maybe you hear knocks, distant laughter, or a comforting word to ease your heart in knowing they are with you.

Closing the Feast

You may find it appropriate to have a special closing ritual after the dinner is done. You may wish to ask everyone around the table to say thank you and a personal message to the spirits in attendance. You may want to ring a bell or share in a song, incantation, or prayer together. Some believe the best way to close the Silent Supper is with a delightful dessert or comforting dinner rolls. However you plan your Silent Supper, know that it is a beautiful ritual to show your appreciation for those you love, miss, and respect.

Planning

Who do you want to honor?

_____

_____

_____

What are their favorites objects and food?

_____

_____

_____

What living guests are you inviting?

_____

_____

_____

Record a Card Pull

DECK USED:

_____

CARD(S) PULLED:

_____

_____

_____

YOUR INTERPRETATION:

_____

_____

_____

_____

_____

_____

BOOK INTERPRETATION:

_____

_____

_____

_____

_____

_____

OCTOBER HERB GUIDE

Herbs for Psychic Ability and Divination

Psychic work and divination are a major aspect of witchcraft, and it's helpful to know which herbs will aid you in your psychic endeavors. The herbs listed above all classify as psychic herbs, each having properties that allow for a range of magical workings. Burn dried yarrow to cleanse your divination tools or create a sacred space.

Create a sachet of amethyst and borage to instill courage when trying a new form of divination, while pennyroyal can be used to prepare yourself for divination or spirit work. Blue vervain added to a bath or made into a tea (use food grade only) will help open your Third Eye and amplify your psychic abilities.

ERB	SIZE/ SPREAD	START SEEDS INSIDE/OUTSIDE	HARDINESS ZONE	NATIVE REGION	GROWTH TYPE**	SUN/ SOIL**
lue rvain	1-2'/1-2'	2-3 mos. (Stratified*) 70° soil/NR	3-10	Wet regions of Missouri	A, P	FS/WD
rrow	6"-3'/2-3'	6-8/After Last Frost	3-9	North America, Europe, Asia	P	FS/LS
rage	1-3'/6-18"	3-4/3-4 After	2-11	Mediterranean	A	PS/R
yroyal	12-18"/18"	8-10/3-4	5-9	Europe, Middle East, North Africa	P	FS,PS/ ML

eks before or afer last spring frost

,=Annual P=Perennial

S= full sun, PS= partial sun; WD= well-drained, M= moist, RM, rich moint, L= loamy, LS=loamy/sandy

Blue Vervain: Known as a psychic herb, associated with the moon. Enhance divination and psychic dreaming
Yarrow: Enhance divination and psychic work, protection against negative energies, prophetic magic, clear blockages, enhance creativity
Borrage: Courage, psychic powers, protection, Air magic
Pennyroyal: Protection of psychic energy against negative influences, strengthen and heal Aura, clear chakra blockages

PAUSE & REFLECT

What common archetype do you most relate to?

_____

_____

_____

_____

_____

_____

_____

_____

_____

_____

_____

_____

_____

_____

_____

_____

_____

_____

OCTOBER FESTIVALS

Dziady is a Slavic holiday concerning the spirits of ancestors that dates back to pre-Christian times. Dziady translates to "Forefathers Eve", the intention of the holiday being communion of the living with the dead or establishing of relationships with the spirits of your ancestors. The holiday of Dziady occurred twice a year: Spring Dziady, from the last day of April to the first day of May, and Autumn Dziady, from the last day of October to the first day of November. It was believed that these were the two days the spirits of the dead were able to return to earth. By establishing yourself as a host, you would secure the favor of the spirit as well as help them find peace once their assistance was no longer required. The ritual of Dziady consisted of eating a feast specially prepared either in your home or at the cemetery on the grave of the spirit you wish to host. While eating, people would drop bits of food and pour some of their drink onto the table or the grave, as offerings for the spirits which you could not clear or remove until the holiday had passed. In some areas the ritual included preparing a bath for the spirit, which was achieved by warming up the sauna or lighting a fire, which provided light to guide them towards you. In modern day practices, this aspect of the ritual is satisfied by lighting candles on the grave.
[Source: https://en.wikipedia.org/wiki/Dziady]

USE THE SPACE BELOW TO RECORD YOUR OCTOBER CELEBRATIONS

OCTOBER

	M	T	W	T	F	S	S
39	25	26	27	28	29	30	1
40	2	3	4	5	6	7	8
41	9	10	11	12	13	14	15
42	16	17	18	19	20	21	22
43	23	24	25	26	27	28	29
44	30	31	1	2	3	4	5

TO DO LIST

-
-
-
-
-
-
-
-
-

DAILY CARD PULL

Monday

Tuesday

Wednesday

Thursday

Friday

Saturday

Sunday

MONDAY 02

TUESDAY 03

WEDNESDAY 04

THURSDAY 05

2023

FRIDAY 06

GOALS

SATURDAY 07

REMEMBER

-
-
-
-
-
-
-

SUNDAY 08

NOTES

HABITS	M	T	W	T	F	S	S

NEXT WEEK

OCTOBER

	M	T	W	T	F	S	S
39	25	26	27	28	29	30	1
40	2	3	4	5	6	7	8
41	9	10	11	12	13	14	15
42	16	17	18	19	20	21	22
43	23	24	25	26	27	28	29
44	30	31	1	2	3	4	5

TO DO LIST

-
-
-
-
-
-
-
-
-

DAILY CARD PULL

Monday

Tuesday

Wednesday

Thursday

Friday

Saturday

Sunday

MONDAY 09 Indigenous Peoples' Da

TUESDAY 10

WEDNESDAY 11

THURSDAY 12

2023

FRIDAY	13		GOALS

SATURDAY	14	● ☀ ♎	REMEMBER

REMEMBER
-
-
-
-
-
-
-

SUNDAY	15		NOTES

HABITS	M	T	W	T	F	S	S	NEXT WEEK

OCTOBER

	M	T	W	T	F	S	S
39	25	26	27	28	29	30	1
40	2	3	4	5	6	7	8
41	9	10	11	12	13	14	15
42	16	17	18	19	20	21	22
43	23	24	25	26	27	28	29
44	30	31	1	2	3	4	5

TO DO LIST

-
-
-
-
-
-
-
-
-

DAILY CARD PULL

Monday

Tuesday

Wednesday

Thursday

Friday

Saturday

Sunday

MONDAY 16

TUESDAY 17

WEDNESDAY 18

THURSDAY 19

2023

FRIDAY	20		GOALS

SATURDAY	21		REMEMBER

REMEMBER
-
-
-
-
-
-
-

SUNDAY	22		NOTES

HABITS	M	T	W	T	F	S	S	NEXT WEEK

OCTOBER

	M	T	W	T	F	S	S
39	25	26	27	28	29	30	1
40	2	3	4	5	6	7	8
41	9	10	11	12	13	14	15
42	16	17	18	19	20	21	22
43	23	24	25	26	27	28	29
44	30	31	1	2	3	4	5

TO DO LIST

-
-
-
-
-
-
-
-
-

DAILY CARD PULL

Monday

Tuesday

Wednesday

Thursday

Friday

Saturday

Sunday

MONDAY 23 ☀♏

TUESDAY 24

WEDNESDAY 25

THURSDAY 26

2023

FRIDAY	27		GOALS

SATURDAY	28	REMEMBER

-
-
-
-
-
-
-

SUNDAY	29	NOTES

HABITS	M	T	W	T	F	S	S	NEXT WEEK

GRATITUDE LIST

MONTHLY TO-DO'S

TRY SOMETHING NEW

CRYSTALS
Ritual tools adorned with the appropriate crystals prove to be much more effective because crystals direct and concentrate energy. For example, enhance your psychic powers by wrapping a string of lapis lazuli beads around a cauldron used for divination; increase the efficacy of a wand used for love magic by adding a rose quartz to the tip. There are limitless options – simply choose crystals whose properties match that of the intention for the tool you'll be using.

CARD SPREAD
Card 1. What I can do for them– Card 2. What they expect of me – Card 3. What I can expect from them

SPELL:
Spell jars are an excellent, easy, way to work magic. They're versatile, so you can make a jar for just about any intention, whether it's love, creativity, money, protection, and so on. Regardless of what you wish to manifest, you'll need the following: small glass jar, cork stopper, tiny scroll of paper and something to write with. The specifics of the next items will vary, depending on what your intention is. If you wish for more money, then a green candle and a gold ribbon would be perfect, whereas an orange candle and yellow ribbon would be better for creativity.
The same goes for herbs and stones – what you'll need will depend on your intent. I always recommend following your instinct, however. If you are making a jar for love, and feel called to add an onyx stone, then add it, even though it's a stone of protection. It could be your intuition telling you to incorporate a bit of protection, so your love doesn't end up hurting you.

ENTITY
Prayer is a powerful tool in devotional practices, but often under-utilized. There are a number of pagan prayer books to learn prayers written for witches, but the best prayers are those which you've written yourself. They don't have to be fancy...they just have to be a sharing of your heart.

SELF-CARE
Write your bucket list – but one that you can & will complete in the next 5 days. Or 5 weeks. The only rules for this bucket list are that they're attainable goals that you want for yourself.

TEA
Tea can help with magic and divination – but have you considered using tea in your devotional practice? Using tea as an offering, or to get yourself into a mindset appropriate for a guided journey, or simple prayer, would be an easy (and delicious) way to forge a relationship with your higher powers.

HERBS
Naturally, this is the perfect time of year to use pumpkins in your magical workings. Pumpkin seeds are excellent for granting wishes and attracting good luck and prosperity. The fruit itself offers protection, repelling malicious energies when carved or inscribed with protective words and/or symbols.

Record a Card Pull

DECK USED:

_____

CARD(S) PULLED:

_____

_____

_____

YOUR INTERPRETATION:

_____

_____

_____

_____

_____

_____

BOOK INTERPRETATION:

_____

_____

_____

_____

_____

_____

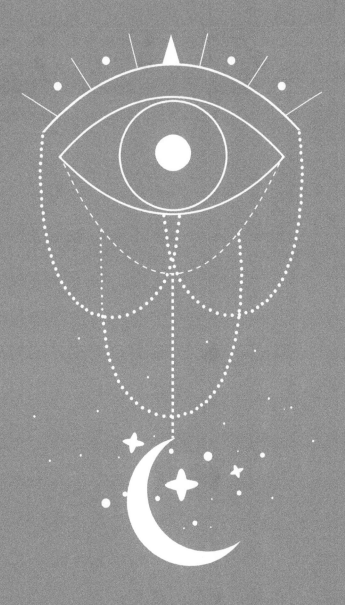

"What's a little love magic between friends?"

- Anna Rowyn

November

OCTOBER

M	T	W	T	F	S	S
30	31					1
2	3	4	5	6	7	8
9	10	11	12	13	14	15
16	17	18	19	20	21	22
23	24	25	26	27	28	29

DECEMBER

M	T	W	T	F	S	S
				1	2	3
4	5	6	7	8	9	10
11	12	13	14	15	16	17
18	19	20	21	22	23	24
25	26	27	28	29	30	31

Goals

Notes

_____
_____
_____
_____
_____
_____
_____
_____
_____
_____
_____
_____
_____

Monday	Tuesday	Wednesday
		1 305/60 — Day of the Dead
6 310/55	**7** 311/54 — Election Day	**8** 312/53
13 317/48 — ♏	**14** 318/47	**15** 319/46
20 324/41 — ♒	**21** 325/40	**22** 326/39 — ♐
27 331/34 — ♊	**28** 332/33	**29** 333/32

NOVEMBER

M	T	W	T	F	S	S
		1	2	3	4	5
6	7	8	9	10	11	12
13	14	15	16	17	18	19
20	21	22	23	24	25	26
27	28	29	30			

Thursday	Friday	Saturday	Sunday
2 306/59	3 307/58	4 308/57	5 309/56
313/52	10 314/51	11 315/50	12 316/49
6 320/45	17 321/44	18 322/43	19 323/42
3 327/38 Thanksgiving Day	24 328/37	25 329/36	26 330/35
0 334/31			

LUNAR PHASES

NOVEMBER 5TH: LAST QUARTER IN LEO

Impressing others and receiving praise will give you a sense of safety and security while the moon is in Leo. This only sets you up for failure, as you'll find yourself at a loss as soon as you're put in the spotlight. The key to navigating through Leo is accepting that feedback and criticism are useful, they help you improve. The first step to accepting these facts is to admit you are afraid of criticism, and to admit that you can't accept criticism. Only once you admit the truth of the problem can you work through it.

NOVEMBER 13TH: NEW MOON IN SCORPIO

Scorpio energy encourages us to explore our feelings more deeply, and we find we're drawn to sex, power and money. Learning what gets other people going is arousing. Instinctive orientation is to start over from scratch. Only by destroying the roots of disturbances can you begin healing.

NOVEMBER 20TH: FIRST QUARTER IN AQUARIUS

The moon in Aquarius gives us the need for emotional freedoms which can cause complications in our relationships. Can also be a time when you are able to better understand your emotions, freeing you from negative feelings such as jealousy, fear, and anger.

NOVEMBER 27TH: FULL MOON IN GEMINI

Under the Gemini moon you may find that communicating your feelings and emotions becomes easier. Your actions are motivated by the desire for variety and the urge to satisfy curiosity. Just be careful you don't become reckless and fickle – the key is harmony of the mind and heart.

RITUAL PLANNER

GOAL/INTENTION:

_____

_____

_____

ITEMS NEEDED:

_____

_____

_____

_____

_____

STEPS:

_____

_____

_____

_____

HEALING CANDLE SPELL

by Luna Aliendro

Candle magic is probably the easiest and most effective form of spell work you can do. Spell candles don't require a lot of supplies, and most of them can be found at your local grocery store. It's perfect for beginners or any witch on a budget.

What you'll need:
· White candle
· Piece of paper
· Rosemary
· Chamomile
· Eucalyptus
· Peppermint

One of the first spells I ever tried was a healing candle. This candle has helped me through so many depressive slumps, times of grief, and flare-ups with my chronic illness. All you need is just a few ingredients. The white light works to cleanse you of illness., while the herbs protect and heal your energy. It may be simple but it's extremely effective.

First, grab a white candle. It can be a chime candle, tealight, or whatever you have on hand. Blend rosemary, chamomile, eucalyptus, and mint together. Take a small amount of the herbs and sprinkle them in a circle around the candle. Then write your name on a piece of paper three times. Turn the paper and write "healing" three times (this should be perpendicular to your name). Fold the paper toward you and place it under the candle. After you light your candle, visualize healing energy flowing through the white light and recite a prayer:

> WHITE LIGHT, SHINING BRIGHT,
> BRING ME HEALING TONIGHT.
> MAGIC MEND AND CANDLE BURN,
> SICKNESS END, GOOD HEALTH RETURN.

As the candle melts, I like to do a quick journaling exercise. Write down what's been troubling you and think of it as removing the issues from yourself and trapping them on the page. If journaling isn't your thing, you could also meditate, draw or paint, then take a bath.

Record a Card Pull

DECK USED:

_____

CARD(S) PULLED:

_____

_____

_____

YOUR INTERPRETATION:

_____

_____

_____

_____

_____

_____

BOOK INTERPRETATION:

_____

_____

_____

_____

_____

PAUSE & REFLECT

If you could go forward 10 years in time to ask your future-self one question, what would you ask?

_____

_____

_____

_____

_____

_____

_____

_____

_____

_____

_____

_____

_____

_____

_____

_____

_____

_____

NOVEMBER FESTIVALS

The northern region of the town Man, located on the Ivory Coast of Africa, plays host to the Festival of Masks. Every November, people from neighboring villages gather together in celebration, dancing and dressed in elaborate masks and colorful costumes. The masks are custom made to embody forest spirits, which are then honored by the dancing and festivities. The neighboring villages hold contests, naming the best dancers. This Festival of Masks is important to the Ivory Coast because it helps unify the region, which has been rife with violence and divided by civil war that has been on-going since 2002. Organizers of the Festival of Masks aim to preserve the culture shared by the diverse population by encouraging unity through the revival of the mask tradition.
[Source: https://www.iexplore.com/articles/travel-guides/africa/cote-divoire/festivals-and-events, https://www.voanews.com/archive/mask-festival-helps-unify-ivory-coast]

USE THE SPACE BELOW TO RECORD YOUR NOVEMBER CELEBRATIONS

NOVEMBER

	M	T	W	T	F	S	S
44	30	31	1	2	3	4	5
45	6	7	8	9	10	11	12
46	13	14	15	16	17	18	19
47	20	21	22	23	24	25	26
48	27	28	29	30	1	2	3

TO DO LIST

-
-
-
-
-
-
-
-
-

DAILY CARD PULL

Monday

Tuesday

Wednesday

Thursday

Friday

Saturday

Sunday

MONDAY 30

TUESDAY 31 Sam

WEDNESDAY 01 Day of the D

THURSDAY 02

2023

FRIDAY 03

GOALS

SATURDAY 04

REMEMBER
-
-
-
-
-
-
-

SUNDAY 05 Daylight Saving Time Ends

NOTES

HABITS

	M	T	W	T	F	S	S

NEXT WEEK

NOVEMBER

	M	T	W	T	F	S	S
44	30	31	1	2	3	4	5
45	6	7	8	9	10	11	12
46	13	14	15	16	17	18	19
47	20	21	22	23	24	25	26
48	27	28	29	30	1	2	3

TO DO LIST

-
-
-
-
-
-
-
-
-

DAILY CARD PULL

Monday

Tuesday

Wednesday

Thursday

Friday

Saturday

Sunday

MONDAY | 06

TUESDAY | 07 | Election Day

WEDNESDAY | 08

THURSDAY | 09

2023

RIDAY	10		GOALS

ATURDAY	11		REMEMBER

REMEMBER
-
-
-
-
-
-
-

UNDAY	12		NOTES

ABITS		M	T	W	T	F	S	S	NEXT WEEK

NOVEMBER

	M	T	W	T	F	S	S
44	30	31	1	2	3	4	5
45	6	7	8	9	10	11	12
46	13	14	15	16	17	18	19
47	20	21	22	23	24	25	26
48	27	28	29	30	1	2	3

TO DO LIST

-
-
-
-
-
-
-
-
-

DAILY CARD PULL

Monday

Tuesday

Wednesday

Thursday

Friday

Saturday

Sunday

MONDAY 13 ● ♏

TUESDAY 14

WEDNESDAY 15

THURSDAY 16

2023

IDAY	17		GOALS

TURDAY	18		REMEMBER

-
-
-
-
-
-
-

NDAY	19		NOTES

BITS		M	T	W	T	F	S	S		NEXT WEEK

NOVEMBER

	M	T	W	T	F	S	S
44	30	31	1	2	3	4	5
45	6	7	8	9	10	11	12
46	13	14	15	16	17	18	19
47	20	21	22	23	24	25	26
48	27	28	29	30	1	2	3

TO DO LIST

-
-
-
-
-
-
-
-
-

DAILY CARD PULL

Monday

Tuesday

Wednesday

Thursday

Friday

Saturday

Sunday

MONDAY 20

TUESDAY 21

WEDNESDAY 22

THURSDAY 23

Thanksgiving Day

2023

RIDAY	24		GOALS

ATURDAY	25		REMEMBER

-
-
-
-
-
-
-

UNDAY	26		NOTES

ABITS		M T W T F S S	NEXT WEEK

NOVEMBER

	M	T	W	T	F	S	S
44	30	31	1	2	3	4	5
45	6	7	8	9	10	11	12
46	13	14	15	16	17	18	19
47	20	21	22	23	24	25	26
48	27	28	29	30	1	2	3

TO DO LIST

-
-
-
-
-
-
-
-
-

DAILY CARD PULL

Monday

Tuesday

Wednesday

Thursday

Friday

Saturday

Sunday

MONDAY 27 ☽ ♊

TUESDAY 28

WEDNESDAY 29

THURSDAY 30

2023

FRIDAY	01		GOALS

SATURDAY	02		REMEMBER

-
-
-
-
-
-
-

SUNDAY	03		NOTES

HABITS	M	T	W	T	F	S	S	NEXT WEEK

GRATITUDE LIST

MONTHLY TO-DO'S

TRY SOMETHING NEW

CRYSTALS:
The vibrant red hue of rubies connects directly with the root chakra, resulting in the person wearing the precious gem feeling more powerful, successful, and proactive.

CARD SPREAD
Card 1. What – Card 2. Why – Card 3. How to Show It

SPELL
Try working with the magic of the stars! Refer to the "Days of the Week" reference section to learn each day's correspondences, and charge your spell with the energy of the sun on the appropriate day.

ENTITY
Study local folklore, learning the beliefs and practices of indigenous peoples who were there before you. Pay particular attention to 'mythical' creatures and entities.

SELF-CARE
Once a week, don't set an alarm clock. Wake up whenever you wake up. No one will think you're lazy or unproductive- you need sleep just as much as the next person.

TEA:
It's possible to be a Tea Witch without having to spend a bunch of money on supplies. Instead of buying a fancy tea infuser, tea filter, tea ball, or tea strainer, you can use coffee filters! Add the tea to the filter, fold it into a pouch, then tie string to the top to close the pouch and provide an easy way to remove the tea leaves. Instead of purchasing a fancy tea kettle, or a tea thermometer, a meat thermometer (they're cheap – just clean it well between uses) and a pot will suffice.

HERBS
Pine trees, along with the rest of the Evergreen family, have always been associated with health and prosperity, due to their ability to withstand the harsh temperatures and conditions of winter when all the other trees have retreated into themselves after the warmth of summer passed. Pine needles especially possess strong cleansing properties, making them suitable for cleaning/cleansing, banishment, as well as healing magic.

Record a Card Pull

DECK USED:

_____

CARD(S) PULLED:

_____

_____

_____

YOUR INTERPRETATION:

_____

_____

_____

_____

_____

_____

BOOK INTERPRETATION:

_____

_____

_____

_____

_____

_____

"Books were my broomstick. They allowed me to fly to other realms where anything was possible."

- Pam Grossman

December

NOVEMBER

M	T	W	T	F	S	S
		1	2	3	4	5
6	7	8	9	10	11	12
13	14	15	16	17	18	19
20	21	22	23	24	25	26
27	28	29	30			

JANUARY

M	T	W	T	F	S	S
1	2	3	4	5	6	7
8	9	10	11	12	13	14
15	16	17	18	19	20	21
22	23	24	25	26	27	28
29	30	31				

Goals

Notes

Monday	Tuesday	Wednesday
4 338/27	**5** 339/26	**6** 340/25
11 345/20	**12** 346/19	**13** 347/18
18 352/13	**19** 353/12	**20** 354/11
25 359/06 Christmas Day	**26** 360/05	**27** 361/04

DECEMBER

M	T	W	T	F	S	S
				1	2	3
4	5	6	7	8	9	10
11	12	13	14	15	16	17
18	19	20	21	22	23	24
25	26	27	28	29	30	31

Thursday	Friday	Saturday	Sunday
	1 335/30	**2** 336/29	**3** 337/28
7 341/24	**8** 342/23	**9** 343/22	**10** 344/21
14 348/17	**15** 349/16	**16** 350/15	**17** 351/14
21 355/10 Yule	**22** 356/09 ☀️♑	**23** 357/08	**24** 358/07 Christmas Eve
28 361/03	**29** 363/02	**30** 364/01	**31** 365/00 New Year's Eve

LUNAR PHASES

DECEMBER 5TH: LAST QUARTER IN VIRGO

The Virgo moon is one of order and practicality. You feel you have to reorganize and bring order to anything you feel is in chaos. This can lead to being intolerant of others, so try focusing more on solving problems, creating order within your life, and helping others without judgement.

DECEMBER 12TH: NEW MOON IN SAGITTARIUS

The moon in Sagittarius is the most optimistic of energies, giving you a craving for new experiences and adventure. Motivations under the Sagittarius moon are driven by the need for the truth, or finding something, be it a philosophy, a goal or new hobby. You may be inclined to overdo things, so make sure you don't forget to count your blessings and appreciate what you have right now.

DECEMBER 19TH: FIRST QUARTER IN PISCES

The moon in Pisces is a great time for a creative or spiritual quest, as the energy heightens your emotional sensitivity and perception of your surroundings. Be mindful of feelings of insecurity. Should you begin to feel insecure just be patient and open to letting events unfold as they come.

DECEMBER 27TH: FULL MOON IN CANCER

The Moon in Cancer instills in you emotional security and a sense of belonging, a sense of nurturing you feel instinctively. You find that you're longing for an intimate connection that's meaningful and long-lasting, enough so you can establish a sense of belonging-put down roots, a place to bunker down as the Universe throws its' trials and tribulations at you. Using the Full Moon energies to work a self-love spell may help to satisfy this desire.

RITUAL PLANNER

GOAL/INTENTION:

_____
_____
_____

ITEMS NEEDED:

_____
_____
_____
_____
_____

STEPS:

_____
_____
_____
_____

NOTES

CUT AND CLEAR SPELL

By Zehara Nachash

We have all been there. A bad breakup. A bad job. We are ready to move on, but there is something there that keeps us holding on. Fear? A chance that maybe things will work out? Whatever it is we cannot quite let go.

But in order for our new spells to work, whether it be to find new love or a better career, we have to be completely rid of the history. You cannot move forward if you're still grounded in the past. That's where a good old cut-and-clear spell comes in.

Cut and clear is exactly what it sounds like. It means cutting the ties that bind you to the old and clearing a path for the new. There is a caveat, however. You have to be 100% ready. There can be no doubt that you are ready to move on. No hesitation that your relationship is really over or that your current job is really not the right one for you. If you are not ready to cut, the clearing will not happen.
You can easily make your own cut-and-clear oil. You will need the following herbs:
- Lemon balm
- Lemon grass
- Eucalyptus
- Rosemary
- Juniper

You can combine all the herbs with a carrier oil, such as olive oil or jojoba, and place them in a dark bottle. Taking a yellow candle, dress it with the oil saying, "All negative energies holding me down are now gone. As this candle burns, so do you weaken." When the candle is burned down, bury the wax in a place where people do not walk. This is you burying the negative energy (or relationship). Walk away and do not look back. You may need to do this several times until you finally feel free from the energy.

You may also do a cut-and-clear bath. Take all the herbs listed and combine them in a bowl with some Epsom salt. As you are soaking, imagine whatever you are holding on to is washing away. Pull the drain and visualize all the negativity going down the drain. If you do not have a bath, take the herbs and place them in a bowl of coconut milk. While standing in the shower, pour the mixture over your head, visualizing the clearing away of all the things you need gone in order to move on.

I always recommend a good cut-and-clear before doing any spell work in which you wish to bring about major changes. It is always good to start fresh!

DECEMBER FESTIVALS

The Iranian festival of Yalda, a celebration of the victory of light and goodness over darkness and evil, takes place on or around December 21st, or the Winter Solstice. According to Persian mythology, the god Mithra, who was born to a virgin mother on the Winter Solstice, symbolizes light, truth, goodness, strength, and friendship. Shab Chera, "night gazing", is honored by modern Persians who observe the holiday by staying up all night. The traditional food of this holiday consists of fruit and nuts, especially pomegranate and watermelon. The red color of these fruits symbolize Mithra and to invoke the crimson hues of dawn. [Source: https://en.wikipedia.org/wiki/Listofmultinationalfestivals_andholidays#December]

USE THE SPACE BELOW TO RECORD YOUR DECEMBER CELEBRATIONS

DECEMBER HERBS

Herbs of Prosperity

Winter is a time of stagnation, darkness, and cold, and so it goes to follow that money can become an issue. December comes with a lot of added expenses, with snow tires, high gas prices, holidays, taking personal days because of weather, heating expenses – the list goes on. But with a simple indoor herb garden containing the above herbs, you will have all you need to ensure your family doesn't struggle this winter. Make sachets, burn as incense, add to cooking, or tuck into decorative wreaths – however you wish to use them, they are sure to protect your family, ease your worries, and keep the cash flowing in.

HERB	SIZE/ SPREAD	START SEEDS INSIDE/OUTSIDE	HARDINESS ZONE	NATIVE REGION	GROWTH TYPE**	SU SOI
Basil	12-24"/ 12"	6-8/ anytime after	10-11	Central Africa, Southeast Asia	A	FS/
Bay Laurel	10-60'/ 5-20	NR	8-10	Mediterranean	TP	FS/
Mint	12-24"/ 18"	NR	4-9	Mediterranean, Asia	P	PS/
Rosemary	4-5'/ 4'	8-10/After	7-10	Mediterranean	TP	FS/

*Weeks before or afer last spring frost

** A=Annual P=Perennial

** FS= full sun, PS= partial sun; WD= well-drained, M= moist, RM, rich moint, L= loamy, LS=loamy/sandy

Magic Properties:
Basil: Money, Wealth, Love, Relationships, Protection
Bay Laurel: Granting Wishes, Manifestation, Prosperity, Protection
Mint: Luck, Money, Healing, Love
Rosemary: Substitute for any herb, Ease Anxiety, Protection, Prosperity, Love, Luck

PAUSE & REFLECT

Go to your first prompt in this planner. You predicted the year, were you correct?

GRATITUDE LIST

MONTHLY TO-DO'S

TRY SOMETHING NEW

CRYSTALS

One thing that I've always believed about crystals is that you find the right one when you are meant to have it – make sure you never miss out on the right crystal by treating yourself to a crystal subscription box. There are many online vendors that offer subscription boxes, each unique in their own way. Check out Etsy, Instagram, Twitter, Facebook – google it, even. There is sure to be a subscription that's perfect for you in price, personality, and products offered.

CARD SPREAD

Card 1: What to give others - Card 2: What to give yourself - Card 3: What to give the world

SPELL

Want to improve the efficacy of your spells? Establish a ritual for working magic. Ritual brings your mind into the present moment, working as a key to 'turn on' or 'get into' the required state of mind. Sasha Graham of "The Magic of Tarot" explains that rituals are a mindfulness practice in which an action aligns with intention. So, by setting up your sacred space, lighting candles, arranging crystals- or whatever you feel compelled to do – you will be performing actions that align with your intention to do magic.

ENTITY

Crone: the aspect of the goddess that embodies feminine energy of experience, wisdom, and insight. As the wise 'elder' (one doesn't actually have to be old to embody the crone) crone deals with transitions of ending – death, break ups, loss of job or home. She is an ally to turn to when you're ready to shed the facades and accept yourself as you are.

SELF-CARE

Write a short story about yourself with supernatural powers. Try to incorporate dramatized versions of real spells you've worked successfully. When life weighs you down, read your story and let your imagination fly high.

TEA

If you're like me, you probably have a difficult time remembering to take your multi-vitamin every day. Now that it's winter-time, it's more important than ever to boost your immune system. If you can't remember to take your vitamins, or if you don't care for the taste of those immunity-boosting drink mixes, turn to tea! Most herbal teas contain antioxidants and a slew of vitamins, and tea vendors often have teas organized by use.

HERBS

Holly is an evergreen shrub that is best known for its' connection to Yule and winter holidays. Holly sprigs will increase happiness, establish balance, and encourage success and good luck for the coming year. The bright red holly berries symbolize the vitalizing blood of the Goddess, creating a connection between the berries, menses, feminine sexuality, and fertility.

DECEMBER

	M	T	W	T	F	S	S
48	27	28	29	30	1	2	3
49	4	5	6	7	8	9	10
50	11	12	13	14	15	16	17
51	18	19	20	21	22	23	24
52	25	26	27	28	29	30	31

TO DO LIST

-
-
-
-
-
-
-
-
-

DAILY CARD PULL

Monday

Tuesday

Wednesday

Thursday

Friday

Saturday

Sunday

MONDAY 04

TUESDAY 05

WEDNESDAY 06

THURSDAY 07
Hanukkah. Begins at Sunse

2023

RIDAY | 08

GOALS

ATURDAY | 09

REMEMBER

-
-
-
-
-
-
-

UNDAY | 10

NOTES

ABITS | M | T | W | T | F | S | S

NEXT WEEK

DECEMBER

	M	T	W	T	F	S	S
48	27	28	29	30	1	2	3
49	4	5	6	7	8	9	10
50	11	12	13	14	15	16	17
51	18	19	20	21	22	23	24
52	25	26	27	28	29	30	31

TO DO LIST

-
-
-
-
-
-
-
-
-

DAILY CARD PULL

Monday

Tuesday

Wednesday

Thursday

Friday

Saturday

Sunday

MONDAY 11

TUESDAY 12 ● ♐

WEDNESDAY 13

THURSDAY 14

2023

RIDAY	15		GOALS

ATURDAY	16		REMEMBER

-
-
-
-
-
-
-

UNDAY	17		NOTES

ABITS		M	T	W	T	F	S	S		NEXT WEEK

DECEMBER

	M	T	W	T	F	S	S
48	27	28	29	30	1	2	3
49	4	5	6	7	8	9	10
50	11	12	13	14	15	16	17
51	18	19	20	21	22	23	24
52	25	26	27	28	29	30	31

TO DO LIST

-
-
-
-
-
-
-
-
-

DAILY CARD PULL

Monday

Tuesday

Wednesday

Thursday

Friday

Saturday

Sunday

MONDAY 18

TUESDAY 19 ☽ ♓

WEDNESDAY 20

THURSDAY 21 Yule

2023

RIDAY	22 ☀♑		GOALS

ATURDAY	23		REMEMBER

- •
- •
- •
- •
- •
- •
- •
- •

UNDAY	24	Christmas Eve	NOTES

ABITS	M T W T F S S	NEXT WEEK

DECEMBER

	M	T	W	T	F	S	S
48	27	28	29	30	1	2	3
49	4	5	6	7	8	9	10
50	11	12	13	14	15	16	17
51	18	19	20	21	22	23	24
52	25	26	27	28	29	30	31

TO DO LIST

-
-
-
-
-
-
-
-
-

DAILY CARD PULL

Monday

Tuesday

Wednesday

Thursday

Friday

Saturday

Sunday

MONDAY 25
Christmas Da

TUESDAY 26

WEDNESDAY 27

THURSDAY 28

2023

RIDAY	29		GOALS

ATURDAY	30		REMEMBER

-
-
-
-
-
-
-

UNDAY	31	New Year's Eve	NOTES

ABITS	M	T	W	T	F	S	S	NEXT WEEK

BOOK OF SHADOWS

A Spell for Wisdom:
- pinch of sage
- dram of whisky
favorite

green witchery

ASTROLOGY 101

REFERENCES

"4 Plant-Inspired Self-Love Practices." Traditional Medicinals. Last updated February 2, 2021, https://www.traditionalmedicinals.com/articles/tea/4-plant-inspired-self-love-practices/

"8 Crystals for Focus & Concentration." Divine Twist. Last Updated October 12, 2021, https://www.divinetwist.com/crystals-for-focus/

"Amazonite Meaning." Energy Muse. Accessed May 23, 2022, https://www.energymuse.com/amazonite-meaning

B, Mae. "Guide to Poultices, Tinctures, and Salves – Quick Guide for at Home Medicine." Medium. March 30, 2020, https://medium.com/@maeb/guide-to-poultices-tinctures-and-salves-quick-guide-for-at-home-medicine-c4bccc76bf6a

Bollinger, Sydney. "5 Herbs to Incorporate into Your New Year's Intentions." Earth Within Flowers. Last updated March 11, 2020, https://earthwithin.com/5-herbs-to-incorporate-into-your-new-years-intentions/.

Cunningham, Scott & David Harrington. The Magical Household: Spells & Rituals for the Home. Woodbury, MN: Llewellyn Publications, 2002.

Eilthireach. "Deeper into Lughnasadh." Order of Bards, Ovates & Druids. December 15, 2019, druidry.org/druid-way/teaching-and-practice/druid-festivals/lughnasadh.

"Festival of Colours." Holi, Society for the Confluence of Festivals in India. 2021, www.holifestival.org/festival-of-colours.html.

"Festival of San Fermín." Wikipedia, Wikimedia Foundation, January 12, 2021, https://en.wikipedia.org/wiki/Festival_of_San_Ferm%C3%ADn

"Fête Du Vodoun." Wikipedia, Wikimedia Foundation. December 23, 2020, https://en.wikipedia.org/wiki/Fête_du_Vodoun

Graham, Sasha. The Magic of Tarot. Woodbury, MN: Llewellyn Publications, 2021.

Gulino, Elizabeth. "This New Moon in Pisces is One of the Most Positive Cosmic Events of the Year." Refinery 29. Last updated February 28, 2022. https://www.refinery29.com/en-us/2022/02/10881555/new-moon-in-pisces-february-2022-meaning-effects

"In the Beginning". "The Early History of Bungee Jumping." Mental Floss, 13 July 2008, www.mentalfloss.com/article/19055/early-history-bungee-jumping.

Jeanroy, Amy. "How to Make Herbal Infusions." The Spruce Eats. Updated April 1, 2022, https://www.thespruceeats.com/how-to-make-an-herbal-infusion-1762142

"June Is LGBT Pride Month." Youth.gov. 2021, https://youth.gov/feature-article/june-lgbt-pride-month

Keates, Sarah. "Damiana: The Love Herb." The Green Goddess. February 15, 2021, https://www.iamthegreengoddess.com/blogs/news/damiana-the-love-herb

"Last Quarter Phase." Zodiac Arts. Accessed April 25, 2022. https://zodiacarts.com/the-cosmos/moon/lunar-cycles/last-quarter-phase/

"Learn How to Garden by the Moon's Phases." Old Farmer's Almanac. Updated March 22, 2022, www.almanac.com/content/planting-by-the-moon.

"The Love Witch- Chocolate Strawberry." Sip a Spell Tea. Accessed April 28, 2022.

https://sipaspell.com/collections/light-half-of-the-year/products/
the-love-witch-chocolate-strawberry

"Moon in Zodiac Sign of Libra." Lunaf. Accessed April 25, 2022.
https://lunaf.com/astrology/moon-in-zodiac/libra/

"Moon Phase Calendar April 2023." AstroSeek. Accessed February 23, 2022.
https://mooncalendar.astro-seek.com/moon-phases-calendar-april-2023

"Moon Phase Calendar August 2023." AstroSeek. Accessed February 23, 2022.
https://mooncalendar.astro-seek.com/moon-phases-calendar-august-2023

"Moon Phase Calendar December 2023." AstroSeek. Accessed February 23, 2022.
https://mooncalendar.astro-seek.com/moon-phases-calendar-december-2023

"Moon Phase Calendar February 2023." AstroSeek. Accessed February 23, 2022.
https://mooncalendar.astro-seek.com/moon-phases-calendar-february-2023

"Moon Phase Calendar: Friday 5th May 2023". Astro-Seek. Accessed April 25, 2022.
https://mooncalendar.astro-seek.com/moon-phase-day-5-may-2023

"Moon Phase Calendar January 2023." AstroSeek. Accessed February 23, 2022.
https://mooncalendar.astro-seek.com/moon-phases-calendar-january-2023

"Moon Phase Calendar July 2023." AstroSeek. Accessed February 23, 2022.
https://mooncalendar.astro-seek.com/moon-phases-calendar-july-2023

"Moon Phase Calendar June 2023." AstroSeek. Accessed February 23, 2022.
https://mooncalendar.astro-seek.com/moon-phases-calendar-june-2023

"Moon Phase Calendar March 2023." AstroSeek. Accessed February 23, 2022.
https://mooncalendar.astro-seek.com/moon-phases-calendar-march-2023

"Moon Phase Calendar May 2023." AstroSeek. Accessed February 23, 2022.
https://mooncalendar.astro-seek.com/moon-phases-calendar-may-2023

"Moon Phase Calendar September 2023." AstroSeek. Accessed February 23, 2022.
https://mooncalendar.astro-seek.com/moon-phases-calendar-september-2023

"Moon Phase Calendar November 2023." AstroSeek. Accessed February 23, 2022.
https://mooncalendar.astro-seek.com/moon-phases-calendar-november-2023

"Moon Phase Calendar October 2023." AstroSeek. Accessed February 23, 2022.
https://mooncalendar.astro-seek.com/moon-phases-calendar-october-2023

"Parrtjima Festival." Tourism Australia, www.australia.com/en-us/events/arts-culture-
and-music/parrtjima-festival.html.

Patterson, Rachel. "Crystal Magic – Bloodstone." Rachel Patterson Author Website. July
21, 2020, https://www.rachelpatterson.co.uk/single-post/crystal-mag
ic-bloodstone

Patterson, Rachel. Kitchen Witchcraft: Garden Magic. Berkeley, CA: Moon Books, 2018.

Patterson, Rachel. "The Magic of Holly and Ivy." Witches & Pagans. December 12, 2017,
https://witchesandpagans.com/pagan-paths-blogs/hedge-witch/the-magic-of-the-
holly-the-ivy.html

Petersik, John. "How To Make A DIY Compost Bin." Young House Love. Updated Janu
ary 2022, www.younghouselove.com/younghouselovedotcompost/ .

"The Piezoelectric Effect." Nanomotion Technology. Nanomotion Johnson Electric
Company, accessed February 1, 2022, https://www.nanomotion.com/nanomo
tion-

technology/piezoelectric-effect/

Raciopi, Jennifer. "Even if This Week Feels Gloomy, the Waning Quarter Moon Means New Beginnings Are Getting Ready To Bloom." Well and Good. February 28, 2021, https://www.wellandgood.com/waning-quarter-moon-sagittarius/

Simonson, Aubrey. "Why You Need to Cold Brew Tea." Good Life Tea. May 23, 2017, https://www.goodlifetea.com/blogs/news/how-to-cold-brew-iced-tea

"Tapati Festival." Easter Island Spirit. February 18, 2021, www.easterislandspirit.com/tapati-festival/.

"Tea Witchcraft." Otherworldly Oracle. March 27, 2019, https://otherworldlyoracle.com/tea-witchcraft/

Todic, Sara. "The Top 5 Crystals for New Beginnings." Lifestyle Blog, Conscious Items. December 28, 2020, https://consciousitems.com/blogs/lifestyle/top-5-crystals-for-new-beginnings-and-how-to-use-them-to-set-intentions.

Vanderlinden, Colleen. "How to Make a Compost Bin Using a Plastic Storage Container." The Spruce. Updated March 19, 2022, www.thespruce.com/compost-bin-from-plastic-storage-container-2539493 .

Wigington, Patti. "Magical Herbal Correspondences." Paganism and Wicca, Learn Religions. Last Updated June 25, 2019, https://www.learnreligions.com/magical-herb-correspondences-4064512.

Willow. "Herbarium: Magical and Medicinal Uses of Holly." Flying the Hedge. December 13, 2015. https://www.flyingthehedge.com/2015/12/herbarium-holly.html

Willow. "Magical Correspondences of Crystals." Flying the Hedge. September 18, 2014. https://www.flyingthehedge.com/2014/09/magical-correspondences-of-crystals.html

"Witch's Cupboard." Sip-a-Spell. Accessed May 23, 2022, https://sipaspell.com/products/witchs-cupboard-chamomile-peppermint

The Witchipedian. "Lapis Lazuli." The Witchipedia, November 28, 2019, https://witchipedia.com/book-of-shadows/minerals/lapis-lazuli/.

The Witchipedian. "Moonstone." The Witchipedia, November 30, 2019, https://witchipedia.com/book-of-shadows/minerals/moonstone/

Witchwood, Leandra. "Magickal Aspects of Basil." The Magic Kitchen. Accessed May 23, 2022, https://www.themagickkitchen.com/magickal-aspects-of-basil/

Witchwood, Leandra. "Magickal Correspondence: Pine." The Magic Kitchen. Accessed March 1, 2022. https://www.themagickkitchen.com/magickal-correspondence-pine/

Witchwood, Leandra. "Pumpkin and Its' Magickal Aspects." The Magic Kitchen. Accessed March 1, 2022. https://www.themagickkitchen.com/pumpkin-magickal-aspects/

AUTHORS

TONYA A. BROWN

TONYA A. BROWN is a current resident of New Orleans, Louisiana, where she is the editor in chief of *Witch Way Magazine* as well as writer and host of the podcast *The Witch Daily Show.* Tonya is a Lenormand reader, medium, and magical guide for other witches. She has spoken at various events including Parliament of the World's Religions, and has written and edited various books on the occult.

✳

Instagram @WitchWayMagazine

AMANDA WILSON

AMANDA WILSON, artist, witch, & SAHM strives to maintain balance between motherhood, witchcraft, and her blossoming career. Amanda's career is an amalgamation of duties: Columnist and Submissions Manager for *Witch Way Magazine*; executive assistant for The *Witch Daily Show* podcast; and content creator, contributing to Medium.com, Vocal. Media, and Hubpages.com. (It's no wonder she is passionate about planners!) To access online profiles or view her writing works, visit Amanda's author's website, www.WriteKindofMagic.art.

WITCH WAY
PUBLISHING